gLAsgow's atLA

Andrew MacCormack

LA 49, above, is seen in Westbourne Gardens, Hyndland on the final day of service 43 operating via this route. The Austin in the foreground of the picture belonged to the photographer. (A. Stirling)

LA 122, below, operated as a mobile ticket office for the Kings Theatre in Glasgow after her withdrawal by GGPTE in late 1977. (D.Cousins)

Cover photo:- *LA 687, which was amongst the last Atlanteans to be delivered to Glasgow Corporation, is seen in Argyle Street in July 1982 during its final weeks of service with the Strathclyde PTE. Two months later the bus was sold to Duncan Stewart Coaches of Dalmuir. (David .G. Wilson)*
Rear Cover:- *Top: LA 284 at Larkfield Garage in as delivered condition. (D.G.Wilson Collection)*
        Bottom: Training bus T2, better known as LA 1399, rests at the Glasgow Bus Museum open day in August 2002. (Author)

 # Contents

Acknowledgements

As always, with a book detailing the history of bus operation, it is impossible for the work to be completed without the help of other people. I hope I have not missed anyone out, but if I have, their omission is purely accidental. The following people have all helped in different ways during the collation of material for this publication, both with the supply of information and the supply of photographs. I hope the photographers are happy with the images I have chosen of their work; many fine and interesting photographs were rejected for the simple reason that they couldn't be accommodated within this publication. So many alterations were carried out on the Glasgow Atlantean fleet that it is impossible to include images of every alteration. Everyone who has helped has been greatly appreciated and words can't fully convey my gratitude to them. The contributors were:-

E. Beaton, D. Brookes, M. Budd, M. Claisse, D. Cousins, A. Douglas, M. Fulton, S. Houston, S. Little, G. Martin-Bates, A. Kerrigan, A. Millar, N Mortson, B. Nicol, S Peebles, A. Potts, B. Ridgway, M. Roulston, D. Rowe, A. Stirling, A. Westwell, D. G. Wilson.

A special thank you to the staff of the German Department at Douglas Academy for translating the message on LA 751.

Thanks also go the staff who are responsible for the archives at Bearsden Library and Dumbarton Library. A large thank you must also go the staff of the Mitchell Library in Glasgow especially the Archives Department and the Glasgow Room. I think a `sorry` is probably in order to the librarians who have had to run down to the basement to find the old *Buses* magazines that were used as a source of information.

A final thank you must go to everyone who kept asking me how the book was coming along. A large amount of data has had to be assessed and as a first time author, I have made mistakes I would avoid in the future. Their promptings have kept me going when it would have been easier to walk away.

As one would expect, a large source of information was pooled in the production of this book and these were:-

A handbook of Glasgow Motorbuses by S. Little, published by STMS, 1970

Almost 50 But Not Quite by S. Little, published by STMS, 1974

Booklet on The Alexander R type Volvo Citybus for wheelchair passengers produced by W Alexander and Strathclyde PTE

British Bus Fleets No. 20 by I. MacLean published by Ian Allan, 1963

British Tram and Trolleybus Systems number ten, Glasgow Buses by S. Little, published by TPC and STMS, 1990

Bus Monograph, Leyland Atlantean by Gavin Booth, published by Ian Allan

Buses Illustrated/ Buses magazine published by Ian Allan

Buses Under Fire by Michael Collins, published by Colourpoint

Glasgow Corporation Transport committee archives 1954– 1973.

GGPTE archives 1973– 1975

Greater Glasgow PTE Annual Reports

Interchange, the GGPTE staff newspaper

100 Years of Glasgow Transport by Brian M. Longworth

Strathclyde PTE Annual Reports

The Daily Record newspaper

The Evening Times newspaper

The Glasgow Bus Museum newspaper

The Glasgow Herald newspaper

The Lennox Herald

The Leyland Atlantean 1958– 1998 by Ron Phillips, published by Gingerfold Publications

The Milngavie and Bearsden Herald newspaper

PSV Circle newssheets

Strathclyde PTE by A. Millar, published Ian Allan.

Strathclyde Passenger Transport Executive published by PSV Circle and The Omnibus Society

Vintage Commercial Vehicles magazine by CMS Publishing

 # Introduction

In March 2002 I decided to put together a book dealing with the Leyland Atlantean bus in Glasgow. I thought that I knew most of the material and that I would struggle to get about 30 pages of content. The evidence suggested that 1501 Atlanteans, almost all of them bodied by Alexanders would not amount to much of a story. Oh boy, I could not have been more wrong! I have spent the last 5 years delving through official documents and other literature unearthing a wealth of information that shows how the Glasgow Corporation Atlantean fleet developed, how the early examples proved troublesome and how their operation was affected by shortages of spare parts, to list a few subjects. It is also interesting to see the first appearance of features that today's Glasgow bus passengers take for granted, cab radios, cash vaults and drivers` security screens for example. The Atlantean fleet spent just under 40 years carrying passengers in Glasgow from 1958 to 1998 and seven were used as training buses for some years after this date with the last one withdrawn in mid 2003. Just as the tram had ruled the first half of the 20th Century, there is no doubt that the Atlantean was as an integral part of Glasgow's environment during the second half of the century. The sad thing is that whilst the tram had a certain appeal to even the man in the street, the Atlantean was just a bus to the vast majority of Glaswegians. They knew its shape, its colour, but not its name. To those of us who loved our `LA s`, the Atlantean was never just a bus, it was THE BUS. As a small boy growing up in the west end of Glasgow in the early seventies, the Glasgow Corporation/ GGPTE fleet just seemed to be teeming with Atlanteans. Saturdays were often shopping days with my parents and trips down Maryhill Road to Kinnairds the greengrocer or Blackadders the butcher were made bearable by the abundance of buses, especially Atlanteans, to be seen. Occasionally a Saturday shopping trip would go down Byres Road and round into Dumbarton Road, where the highlight, apart from the trip on the number 1 bus, was the opportunity to see all these buses going to strange faraway places like Auchenshuggle, Cathcart, Hillington and Keppochill Road instead of the usual Carmyle, Shettleston and Tollcross. Even in those days the roar of the Atlantean and those front entrance doors made these buses stand out from anything else in the fleet. The book is divided into two main sections. The first deals with the idiosyncrasies of the buses themselves and for this the buses are described in the batches that they were ordered. The second section of the book deals with important periods of the Atlantean`s service in Glasgow. I hope you have as much enjoyment reading the book as I did researching it.

Andrew MacCormack, April 2007

Designed and printed by **April Sky Design**
Colourpoint House
Jubilee Business Park
21 Jubilee Road
Newtonards
County Down
Northern Ireland
BT23 4YH

028 9182 7195

How it all started : LA 1

At the 1956 Earls Court Show a prototype bus, 281 ATC, was exhibited that ultimately would have a major impact on the British bus scene for the next 40 years. Successors to this bus would help to introduce one man operation, OMO, to Britain. In 1956 someone had come up with the revolutionary idea of placing the engine at the wrong end of the bus, the rear. Today it does not seem that revolutionary but it has to be remembered that in 1956 the half cab bus reigned supreme in the bus world, London Transport's first AEC Routemaster had been delivered only two years before. However in 1956 Glasgow buses were not the only passenger carrying vehicles that used the Queen's highway. The trams were still running and would continue to run on a contracting network for another six years. There were also trolleybuses and Glasgow's 'silent death' outlasted the trams before their withdrawal in 1967. 281 ATC was the very first Atlantean , of thousands, that Leyland would produce over the next 28 years and although this bus did not operate in Glasgow, officials from the Corporation inspected it.

It must have made an impression because the Corporation's transport committee considered in August 1956 whether to buy an Atlantean. The committee were told the bus could be delivered by New Years Day 1957 and it would seat 78 with 8 standees. Not only that, the chassis could be bodied by either MCW or Alexanders of Stirling. In a written submission to the transport committee, Eric Fitzpayne, Glasgow Corporation's transport manager, told

them that one bus should be purchased for trial purposes as in his opinion it was likely to be the bus of the future. As history shows, the purchase was approved with the bus arriving in late 1958.

At the 1958 Earls Court Show there were four production Atlanteans, chassis type PDR 1/1, on display. Three of the buses had MCW bodies:- FHF 451 Wallasey Corporation No1, RTH 637 James of Ammanford No 227 and 43 DKT Maidstone and District DL 43. The fourth bus, chassis number 582374 is the bus that interests us. Bodied by Alexanders, it had an H44/34F body and came at a finished cost of £6150. The bus had a number of `firsts` associated to it. Alexanders had not previously exhibited in the Capital under it's own name and the bus also carried the first body finished at the then new Falkirk factory after the company had moved there from Stirling. Alexanders would body over 2500 Atlanteans for the UK market alone before the chassis was replaced by the Leyland Olympian. In keeping with Alexander tradition, the bus did not carry a registration number at Earls Court.

The bus was delivered to Glasgow Corporation, GCT, on the 26th November 1958 and was registered FYS 998 from the transport department's exclusive series, gaining fleet number LA 1. The Glasgow Herald newspaper reporting 'Glasgow test bus with automatic door' and that LA 1 was the 'largest bus in Glasgow'. On the 15th December 1958 it entered service from Ibrox Garage on service 4,

Preserved LA 1 in attendance at the Larkfield Depot open day in April 1978. The bus by this time had been fitted with a different style of side lights and front fog lights to those it had earlier in its career. (D. Cousins)

Balornock—Drumoyne. Initially its livery was cream roof and upper windows, bus green between decks, cream lower deck windows and orange lower deck panels. Of the four production examples, arguments rage about which entered service first. LA 1 had been the first chassis released from the Leyland works, but it missed being the first Atlantean into service by a matter of days, the Wallasey or James Atlantean are the two candidates for that honour.

Compared with the following 1448 Atlanteans that were bought new, LA 1 was non standard in several respects. The most obvious feature being its flat, almost box shape with split windscreen and there was no side number box. At the rear it had a one piece engine cover, indicators on either side of the lower saloon rear window and the heating grilles were in the recess above the engine cover. Internally the bus had a flat floor from the front platform to the edge of the rear axle where a step was placed to lift the floor over the axle. It was delivered with a Leyland 0.600, 9.8 litre/ 6 cylinder engine of 125 b.h.p., centrifugal clutch and Pneumo-cyclic gearbox with electric gearchange on the steering column. In plain English it was a semi automatic, i.e. the driver selects the gears as he would in a manual vehicle, but he does not have a clutch pedal in the cab. On overhaul the bus was converted to mark two Atlantean type with fluid friction clutch and 3 piece engine cover. The rear indicators were panelled over and the heating grilles were moved to either side of the rear number plate.

Although the first rear engine bus in the GCT fleet, it was not the first front entrance bus, the Corporation having already bought 30 Leyland Royal Tiger Worldmaster saloons. LA 1 was never converted for OMO and during it's career operated from Ibrox, Knightswood and Partick Garages. Placed in storage at Knightswood in February 1973, it was reactivated in April that year as a driver trainer at the same garage. By late 1974 it had been delicensed and was in Bridgeton Garage on behalf of the Museum of Transport who planned to preserve the bus. On the closure of Bridgeton the bus moved to Langside Garage. Currently residing in the Museum of Transport in the former Kelvin Hall, LA 1 carries the livery used between 1959 and 1973 of bus green upper half and orange lower half separated by a cream band. Considering the bad luck encountered by the first examples of the vehicles bought since, it is all the more remarkable that LA 1 is still with us. Although a museum exhibit, LA 1 has occasionally returned to the streets of the city over the years, an example being the Atlantean farewell in June 1998.

Delivered with a Leyland badge below the front windscreen depicting Atlas holding the globe, LA 1 later acquired a `Leyland Albion St Andrews` badge. At the present time the bus has reacquired its original badge below the windscreen.

Despite its revolutionary concept and successful operation, LA 1 initially remained unique in the Glasgow fleet. Traditional rear entrance Leyland Titan and Daimler CVG 6 as well as front entrance Titan and AEC Regent 5 were bought in the 1959 - 61 period. The lack of Atlantean purchases however did not mean that interest in the chassis had subsided.

In October 1961 Mr Fitzpayne, the Chief Engineer Mr Shaw, the convener and sub convener of the transport committee as well as Councillor Walter Miller all travelled south of the border to visit the Leyland plant at Leyland and the spare parts factory at Chorley. During the visit they were shown round the workshops and given the opportunity to inspect the manufacturing of various parts that constitute the bus chassis, Leyland even providing a Liverpool Atlantean for inspection by the party. Two features caught their attention, grab handles on either side of the entrance which came at an extra cost of £6 per bus and the flat floor in the Liverpool Atlantean. Unlike LA 1, this bus had a flat floor from the rear of the vehicle to the front edge of the staircase, with a step down onto the platform.

The undoubted highlight of the trip was a ride along the M6 motorway in a Ribble Atlantean that was provided by Leyland. This bus with its air suspension on the front axle and ability to attain 55mph must have been quite an eye opener. When reporting back to the transport committee, Mr Fitzpayne mentions, `the ride qualities were excellent and there is no doubt that air suspension is superior to the conventional leaf spring layout,` as used in Glasgow. The air suspension added £ 106 to the cost of the chassis, however, and what pre-motorway Glasgow would have done with a 55 mph Atlantean in 1961 is also open to question.

The visit certainly proved productive as Mr Fitzpayne felt that grab handles should be added to the fleet and they were retrofitted to LA 1. Despite the significant advantages of the Liverpool platform/saloon layout, this was a departure he could not recommend. LA 1 was displayed to members of the transport committee in its manufactured form and with a wooden mock up of the Liverpool arrangement. Despite this, some members still had doubts and to answer these Liverpool Corporation Atlantean E2, 372 BKA, visited the City Chambers in early November 1961. It and LA 1 were then displayed to the transport committee so they could get a visual comparison of the two buses.

LA 2—102

LA 2-102 SGD 580—680 Leyland PDR 1/1 Alexander H44/34F
101 buses delivered between August 1962 and March 1963.

The next Atlanteans to arrive, LA 2-102 at a complete cost of £ 6 700, commenced on the 17th of August 1962 with LA 4. Carrying the simplified spray painted livery, for a short period of time Atlanteans and trams shared Glasgow's streets. LA 2 would be the only Atlantean, apart from LA 1, to carry the cream band above the front windscreen, although this feature was subsequently removed from LA 2.

The final tram route, 9 Auchenshuggle– Dalmuir West, ceased on the 1st of September 1962 being replaced by bus route 64 from the following day. On the 4th of September ` the last tram procession` snaked its way through the city, with LA 20 hidden in amongst the tramcars. Electric traction would continue on the city's streets for another five years until the trolleybus system was abandoned. Whilst some of this batch did replace trams, it would be wrong to label the whole batch ` tram replacement vehicles`. It had been forecast that 56 new buses would be needed to cover the trams by September 1962 with a further 20 replacing elderly buses in the fleet. The dominance of the Atlantean in the GCT fleet over the next 11 years can be seen in the fact that when GGPTE took over the bus fleet on the 1st of June 1973, Atlantean deliveries had reached LA 695. The grand total of other chassis delivered during this period was 17, 1 Daimler Fleetline and 16 Leyland Panther saloons.

LA 4 introduced a new, more attractive style of Alexander body than the one used previously on LA 1, later to be known as the `Glasgow style Alexander body`. With the upper front windscreen bearing similarities to the rear of the Alexander `Y` type body and a large curved driver's windscreen, this body subsequently became the standard Alexander body style for both Atlanteans and Daimler Fleetlines. The new bodywork was 30 feet 8 inches long, longer than the previous permitted maximum by 8 inches. Thus it was that several GCT Atlanteans from this batch spent time as demonstrators with other operators. LA 6 got sent to Coventry, home of the Daimler factory, for a week in August 1963 operating service 8 to Tile Hill Village. After trials that were reported successful, Coventry contentiously ordered 22 Atlanteans in 1964. LA 6 was withdrawn damaged in June 1972 at Newlands Garage by GCT. Although included in the transfer of vehicles to GGPTE the next year, LA 6 would not run again. LA 83 was another Atlantean that spent time on loan, operating with Birkenhead in early January 1963 then passing to Lincoln before spending two weeks at Stockon.

LA 2—102 were Mark 2 Atlanteans with Leyland 0.600 ` Semi power plus` engines of 125 b.h.p., fluid friction couplings, pneumo-cyclic gearboxes and electric gearchange on the steering column. These buses also had

Seen passing a GCT Fare Stage indicator in George Square when almost new is LA 22. Whilst the new style of body that Alexanders put on these buses draws the eye in, other visible features of note are grab-handles on the front platform, the `Leyland Albion` badge on the front dash and the double curvature one piece driver's windscreen. (D.G. Wilson collection)

three piece engine hoods of which only the centre opened. From new these buses had grab handles on either side of the entrance, side number boxes, hopper window vents and fluorescent lighting. As with LA 1, the heater vents remained under the rear canopy.

Heat, or rather lack of it, had been a bone of contention for crews throughout Britain during the fifties and early sixties. In Glasgow, Ibrox Garage walked out over the issue in early January 1962. 300 staff at Ibrox walked out on the 8th of January after complaining that the buses based there were inadequately heated. The problem at Ibrox being compounded by the garage being open air with none of its buses under cover. During the cold weather in January 1962 the buses had been like ice boxes. The Ibrox staff were not alone in this grievance and throughout the 8th, crews at Langside, Newlands and Possilpark Garages joined the walkout. By the evening rush hour 500 buses were off the road. To emphasise the point, it is worth noting that only 141 buses had saloon heaters, 66 had cab heaters and 86 had demisters at the time of the strike. LA 2 –102 and future Atlanteans would represent significant improvements in comfort in a city that can suffer from cold temperatures at any time of the year, the buses being fitted from new with saloon and cab heaters as well as demisters. LA 2 also introduced the `Leyland Albion Atlantean ` badge which was fitted front and rear on all Atlanteans until LA 500 and a few above this mark as well. The reason behind the badge was to give these English built buses a Scottish feel. Some chassis intended for Glasgow ended up being delivered elsewhere and at least two examples were delivered to English operators. UWH 192 was delivered to Bolton, as it's 192, and carried the first East Lancs body on an Atlantean and was also the first Atlantean to have engine shrouds fitted to the body. XWU 890G was delivered to T. Severn and Sons Limited of Dunscroft near Doncaster in 1969. This later chassis receiving a Roe body.

After withdrawal from Glasgow, most of the batch either went straight for scrap or to small independents for further use. LA 93 was withdrawn by GGPTE in 1978 and sold to Westway Coaches of Newquay around May of that year, the new owner taking the roof off the bus and converting it to O44/34F configuration. The bus was then used in this format until it's withdrawal in October 1979.

Such was the popularity of Glasgow Atlanteans, that Leyland bought LA 91 from GCT and LA 202 was added onto the next batch of Atlanteans as its direct replacement. It is believed that LA 91 never operated for GCT, but it did see use in Glasgow. A few of the many operators to try LA 91 were Halifax, Rotherham Corporation, Trent, Wallasey Corporation and Western SMT. Painted in a yellow and cream livery, similar to the livery used by Newcastle Corporation, the bus carried side adverts stating,` This is the ` LEYLAND ATLANTEAN 78 seater `. It spent 2 weeks during March 1964 on Tyneside during which time the operator also had Alexander bodied Fleetline demonstrator 565 CRW on loan. This latter bus had been the bus that Glasgow had refused to buy from Alexanders. LA 91 went for 3 weeks of trials with Halifax from mid May 1964, competing with buses from the local fleet as well as other demonstrators. Halifax was keen to find a bus that was suited to this hilly part of West Yorkshire. After spending 3 weeks operating a week at a time on one of three routes common to all demonstrators Halifax's General Manager, Geoffrey Hilditch, commented that, ` Generally speaking our staff and passengers were pleased with its performance.` Despite the engine producing 125 b.h.p.,

The bottom of Jamaica Street and a well presented LA 79, sporting GGPTE livery, has just left the cavernous terminus under Central Station that was Midland Street for Govan Cross. (David.G. Wilson)

Halifax felt that the bus was slightly underpowered. The braking system on LA 91 was noted for its smoother stops than the Fleetline demonstrator and its fuel consumption was better as well. Also on loan to Halifax as part of the trials was a Wallasey Atlantean, but it did not fare as well as LA 91. The former Glasgow Atlantean had the second best fuel consumption, 9.45 mpg, of all trial buses and also took second place in a maintenance tasks trial to an AEC Routemaster. Disappointment was to follow for both AEC and Leyland. In the aftermath of the trials Halifax ordered five Dennis Lolines and later followed these with five Leyland Titan PD 2s and then Daimler Fleetlines.

LA 91's demonstration period with Western SMT in early January 1965 is also of interest. Western had a Fleetline demonstrator, 4559 VC, on loan and used the bus on the long Ayr to Dumfries service. LA 91 joined the Fleetline on this route for a week of comparative trials. The following week both buses were moved to the Ayr to Glasgow via Paisley route. Thus the bus did see passenger service in Glasgow, but it would have been interesting to see the reactions of the Paisley public to a Western SMT bus that externally must have looked like a Grahams of Paisley vehicle.

Leyland was keen for the Atlantean to sell on the European mainland and LA 91 travelled to Paris complete with `C`est un Leyland Atlantean, le 78 seater` adverts replacing the identical English version. Of course the bus wasn't able to operate in France due to it being right hand drive, but left hand drive Atlanteans were sold to Portugal. After finishing demonstration work with Leyland, LA 91 was sold to well known Lancashire independent J. Fishwick and Sons who over the years have taken several former Leyland demonstrators. Now numbered 34, LA 91 remained internally similar to its sisters just over 200 miles to the north. In the spring of 1978 the bus was sold to another Lancashire Independent, Mercers of Longbridge.

October 1972 finds SGD 669 parked in a corner of Fishwick`s Garage in Leyland. Note that the `Albion Atlantean` badge that was standard on all GCT PDR chassis has been changed for a `Leyland Atlantean` badge. (D. Cousins)

LA 103–202

LA 103–151 SGD 681—729 Leyland PDR 1/1 Alexander H44/34F
LA 152–161 SGD 731—740 Leyland PDR 1/1 Alexander H44/34F
LA 162-202 AGA 101-141B Leyland PDR 1/1 Alexander H44/34F
100 buses delivered between August 1963 and October 1964.

To allow outstanding orders of buses for Midland Red and the Scottish Bus Group to be completed at Alexanders, there was a cessation in deliveries to GCT until August 1963 after LA 102 arrived in December 1962. LA 103– 202 themselves saw only minor detail changes from the previous batch with an extra interior light added in the upper rear dome and the heater intake grilles relocated to either side of the rear number plate. This latter modification being made necessary because exhaust fumes were entering the heating system when the intake grilles were above the engine cover.

Another bus used to extol the benefits of the Leyland Atlantean was LA 138 which went on loan to CIE of Ireland in 1964. This bus was one of four demonstrators that Leyland provided to C.I.E. in the 1961-4 period before C.I.E. decided to purchase Atlanteans, with deliveries starting in 1966. The Corporation was happy to send the bus as long as the costs of delivering the bus to Dublin and returning it to GCT were met by Leyland. C.I.E on the other hand would have to fit their own tyres to LA 138 and pay for the hire of the bus during the time it was in Dublin. During its demonstration period, C.I.E. used the bus on Dublin cross city route 10, Phoenix Park to Donnybrook.

LA 138 was also involved in the Christmas 1964 Glasgow city tour. The story of its involvement begins in the autumn of 1964 with a pay dispute. Nationally the drivers` union had applied for substantial improvements to their members` working conditions, including a substantial pay rise, a reduction in the working week to 40 hours and an incentive scheme. As part of the attempt to force the Corporation's hands, GCT crews banned overtime for two weeks from the 22nd November. Unfortunately for GCT, this coincided with their plans to start an evening tour of the city centre Christmas lights. The theory behind the tour was simple enough. Each year several of the streets in the city centre were decorated with lights for the Christmas period and GCT thought that an evening bus tour run along these streets would allow the public to view the attractions in comfort. A tour schedule was produced and LA 138 was chosen as the tour bus with pink lights used to illuminate the saloons. Retaining GCT livery, but with the between decks panels painted white, suitably sign written and illuminated by external lights the bus took to the streets on the 7th December departing Saint Enoch Square at half hourly intervals from 7pm until 9.30 pm. Due to the overtime ban the tour only ran for three weeks instead of the intended five weeks. If the tour had been a commercial success, LA 148 would have been used as a duplicate bus. Unfortunately for GCT, the public were not so keen about

the tour and LA 148 rarely saw use. Although revenue just about covered expenses, GCT was disappointed with the returns. It was felt that for the public to get a good view of the lights, passengers had to get an upstairs seat and consequently this affected patronage. None the less, the tour returned the following year and ran from 22nd November until 30th December on weekday evenings with departures revised to operated half hourly from 7pm till 9pm The 1965 tour made an even greater loss than the previous year and it was no great surprise when the tour failed to appear in 1966.

The registration numbers of this batch is intriguing. The allocation of SGD 730 to GCT`s sole Daimler Fleetline, D268, that arrived in May 1963 led to the sequence jumping between LA 151 and LA 152. The final allocation from Glasgow's exclusive registration number series, SGD 740, went to LA 161 and had suffixes not been introduced in Glasgow during 1964, then registrations up to SGD 949 would have been allocated to buses; SGD 950 –999 having been left for use on support vehicles. Indeed, registrations as high as SGD 781 had been discussed for the batch up to LA 202, although ultimately this was academic, the reason being the delivery of LA 162, AGA 101B, which had the first suffix registration plate on a GCT bus. LA 162– 5 had in fact been noted at Alexanders prior to delivery carrying SGD 741- 4 although by the time of their delivery run, the registration plates had been changed to AGA 101– 4B.

LA 202 was more than a direct replacement for LA 91. In early October 1963 Grahams of Paisley bought a new Alexander bodied Atlantean, number 61 (HXS 65), that had actually been built on a chassis destined for GCT. Thus when LA 202 was built in 1964 it used the chassis that had originally been intended for the Grahams bus.

Several of this batch were to attract interest after withdrawal, although the first bus, LA 111, is more notable for the reason of its demise. The Bridgeton based bus was stolen in August 1974 and when recovered was missing the majority of its upper deck after having been driven through a low bridge. The bus was delicensed at its home garage and was eventually sold to a Barnsley dealer in February 1976. It is more than likely that the bus was kept as a source of spares rather than for a possible return to service.

LA 122 was transferred to Glasgow District Council, Halls Department, in December 1977, painted Day-Glo yellow and given signwriting for the Kings Theatre, Glasgow. As part of its livery, cartoon characters were painted on the sides of the bus muttering finest Glasgow patter. The Halls Department used the bus as a radio controlled booking office until its withdrawal in 1981.

LA 125 was another bus that lost it's roof after leaving Glasgow, being acquired by Dodsworth of Minskip in May 1976 via a Barnsley dealer. The bus was sold back to the dealer in December 1979 and then sold, in April 1980, to Holt`s Coaches of Newport as a non psv open topper. By August of 1980, the bus had reacquired its roof and was sold to Kenmarga Coaches in December 1980. The bus being sold to a dealer in August 1981 and scrapped in November 1981.

LA 149 was sold to Grampian Regional Transport in March 1976 where it was renumbered 91 and used as a driver trainer until its withdrawal in April 1982.

LA 183 and LA 188 were sold to English dealers before ending down under in Australia on the Northern New South Wales Coast in 1976 for use as school buses. LA 183 was purchased by Port Macquarie Bus Service and was reregistered MO 4675 with fleetnumber 18 allocated to it. The bus gained large ventilation panels between the front headlights and also where the destination box had previously been.

LA 188 was bought byWreight, New Brunswick, New South Wales, registered MO 7714 and was later sold to Jarvis of Brunswick during 1978. A large bumper was fitted on the front panel of the bus and both LA 183 and 188 had their side indicators relocated to the front panel. Another antipodean feature was the placing of small lights just above the lower windscreen.

LA 184 had its engine removed in May 1976 and was repainted all–over Verona green, the bus then finding use as a shop–steward's office at Larkfield Garage. In September 1981, the bus was moved to Ibrox Garage for disposal.

LA 186 was taken over by GGPTE in June 1973 as a withdrawn vehicle, having been delicensed because of fire damage in May 1973 whilst allocated to Ibrox Garage. The bus was later transferred to Knightswood Garage, no doubt to sit in the infamous graveyard. By June 1975, LA 186 had been stripped for spares and was disposed of to the Barnsley scrapyards in February 1976.

LA 193–202 were the first new vehicles to be allocated to Partick Garage when it reopened as a bus garage on the 4th October 1964. Operating services 9,15,63 and 64, the garage had previously operated trams for the Corporation until the 2nd June 1962. Other Atlanteans that were transferred in time for the opening were LA 1-3/6-8/10/13-26/28-31/83/4/86-9 from Knightswood and LA 118 from Possilpark.

The external lights that were fitted to LA 138 for the Christmas Lights tour are just above Santa`s head on the front nearside between decks panel. (David.G. Wilson Collection)

LA 203–284

LA 203–221 AGA 142– 160B Leyland PDR 1/1 Alexander H44/34F
LA 222–242 CYS 568– 588C Leyland PDR 1/1 Alexander H44/34F
LA 243–284 DGE 280– 321C Leyland PDR 1/1 Alexander H44/34F
82 buses delivered between October 1964 and December 1965.

By January 1964 the Corporation was looking to replace 124 Regent Mark 3, 36 of which were new in 1948 and the other 88 were new in 1949, and 38 Daimler CVD 6 which were new in 1949. All were due to have their Certificate of Fitness renewed during 1964/5 and to keep the buses on the road would have required an overhaul of each vehicle. With this in mind, GCT decided it would be better to buy new buses and invited tenders for the supply of 162 bus chassis. The following quotes were received in response to the Corporation's request:-

to supply Leyland Atlanteans at £2923 per chassis
to supply Leyland Atlanteans with drop centre axle at £3123 per chassis
to supply Daimler Fleetlines at £ 3307 per chassis
to supply Leyland Titan PD3A/2 at £ 2861 per chassis
to supply AEC Renowns at £ 3185 per chassis
to supply AEC Regents, Mark 5, at £ 2911 per chassis

Leyland also quoted the Albion Lowlander chassis, which was built locally at its Scotstoun Works. GCT had taken one, 747 EUS, on extended loan for nearly a year from March 1962. Mr Fitzpayne clearly wasn't taken with the bus when he told the transport committee that, `It is a lowbridge bus and our experience shows it is unsuited to Glasgow conditions.` It is interesting to note that Leyland was still trying to sell Titans to GCT, only £ 62 per chassis cheaper than an Atlantean, when it had already sold the Corporation 200 Atlanteans. Mr Fitzpayne also informed the transport committee that should a front engined bus be considered, then only the AEC Renown would be suitable. At a cost of £ 3185 , dearer than the 78 seat Atlantean by £ 262, it was no surprise that Atlanteans were chosen as the winning tender, LA 203– 364.

The first Atlanteans of this order started to arrive before the year was out and as usual carried Alexanders bodywork. It would be wrong to assume that the proximity of Falkirk to Glasgow had a bearing on the choice of bodywork. For this batch MCW had bid for the bodybuilding contract, although at £ 40 per chassis dearer than Alexanders, there was no question of the bodies not being built in Falkirk. Although Alexanders were still bodying the buses, a new shape of bus was apparently under consideration. Correspondence on the matter is scarce, but Alexanders wrote to Mr Fitzpayne in February 1964 regarding the appearance of the Atlantean at the rear having apparently thoroughly investigated the possibility of enclosing the space above the bonnet. They explained to Mr Fitzpayne that Potteries Motor Traction, PMT, had taken an Atlantean with bodywork from a different manufacturer in 1963 with an enclosed rear bonnet. This bus subsequently gave considerable trouble to its owner. Alexanders explained that in its current order for 25 buses for PMT, the company clearly instructed Alexanders, `not to attempt to close in the rear.` PMT had found that the weight of the engine cantilevered at the rear, made it impossible to successfully tie body framing to the bonnet cover. Glasgow's Atlanteans therefore received only minor bodywork changes at the rear until the arrival of the AN 68s with shrouds in 1973. CIE of Ireland on the other hand enclosed the engine compartment on all of its Atlanteans right from the first one delivered in 1966.

Fibreglass bumpers at the base of the engine compartment were a new addition with this batch, a feature subsequently retro-fitted to previous deliveries. Another feature that made its debut towards the end of this batch were small round front Indicators that were located immediately below the side lights.

Vehicles of note from this batch include:-

LA 208 which was sold to Fabergee Promotions in 1977 for use as a mobile showroom. The bus was later sold to Moodie of Haselmere who partially converted it to open top configuration for used as a hospitality unit.

LA 220 was involved in the darkest incident to befall any of the Atlantean fleet. On a Saturday evening in February 1968 the bus was on its last run of the day, a short turn to its home garage at Partick. Around 1135pm a gang of youths, who were passengers on the bus, were involved in a serious incident involving a member of the crew. Outraged crews at all 12 of the Corporation's garages made their anger at the incident known by staging 8pm curfews of services to force the Corporation into action on the issue of bus crew security. The crews at Partick continued their curfews after other garages had returned to normal working. The Corporation's solution was to begin immediately installing `anti thug` Klaxons at a cost of £36 000 in the buses in event of the crew being attacked. The use of two way radios on the buses was also expanded, with radio fitted buses allocated to all GCT garages and used where they were most needed. LA 220, not surprisingly, was blacked by crews at Partick after the incident and later the bus was moved to another garage.

Initially sold to Carlton Metals of Barnsley in 1977, LA 232 had made it to Japan by 1984 where it was being used by the Restaurant Huya as an immobile publicity vehicle. Unfortunately, it had been painted into London Transport livery, complete with gold London Transport fleetnames.

Well known as the open topper that never was is LA 243. In 1970 the bus was allocated to Partick Garage when it was decapitated trying to gain access to Castlebank Street.

Apparently its driver had tried in vain to take the bus under the low railway bridge close to where the old Partick Fire Station stood. I understand the bus was damaged from around the height of the destination box upwards. Sent to Larkfield Bus Works for repair, the bus was initially converted to open top configuration The reason for this being Celtic`s progress to the 1970 European Cup Final in Milan. In 1967 after after `the Bhoys` historic 2-1 triumph over Inter Milan in Lisbon, the team had to do their victory parade through Glasgow on the back of a coal lorry. To avoid a repeat of this spectacle in 1970, the Corporation had LA 243 prepared. As usual in football, the only predictable thing is the unpredictability and `the Hoops` duly lost the Final 2-1 to Feyenoord of Holland. With no other use for an open top bus the roof was put back onto LA 243 and it returned to service without having been used in open top form.

In October 1976, LA 253 had its body removed at the Bus Works as part of its preparation as a training aid. After its body was removed, the chassis and all remaining parts were cleaned prior to colour coding of each of its separate systems, e.g. air, electrics, fuel, etc. The colour system indicating the various working systems and this helped apprentices to develop a clear understanding of how a bus works. Prior to the bus arriving, apprentices had lacked opportuniiess to gain the relevant experience.

By January 1978, LA 269 had found its way to the Scottish Arts Council. for use as a mobile art gallery. Rebodied by Bennett of Glasgow, the bus was fitted with a new, almost, box shape body with only the front dash and driver's windscreen remaining from the previous body. Interestingly, during the modifications the engine compartment was enclosed to allow the gallery to be used for exhibitions and a display area with floor space 22 feet by 8 feet which allowed a wide variety of exhibitions to be displayed was created. The gallery had started in 1978 as a pilot scheme in the Scottish Borders and such was its success that it soon appeared in other regions. The gallery's mobility allowed it to take a high standard of exhibits to outlying communities whose populace would otherwise have to visit a large city like Edinburgh or Glasgow to see similar exhibits. By the end of 1980 it was believed to have been visited by 30 000 people. The former LA 269 visited the Borders, the Lothians, Dumfries and Galloway as well as the Highlands of Scotland including Skye. Whilst with the Scottish Arts Council, the bus was used as a mobile art gallery and was believed to have been withdrawn in 1983 when the Scottish Arts Council bought a new Leyland Olympian to continue this work. LA 269 when last heard of several years ago was in an Aberdeenshire scrapyard.

LA 284 was the undoubted star of this batch. Prior to entering service, the bus appeared at the International Transport Exhibition in Munich in 1965. Leyland was particularly keen to appear at the exhibition, but as it was not covered by the Society of Motor Manufacturers, Leyland could not directly apply for exhibition space. Instead Leyland asked GCT to apply for the space with the manufacturer making it quite clear that they would pay for all the financial and other responsibilities involved. In preparation for its trip abroad, the bus gained non standard yellow wheels and `GB` plates, which it retained for some time after returning home. Whilst in Munich, the bus was used to carry passengers to and from the exhibition. Internally, LA 284 was the only member of this batch to have a ramped floor instead of the usual step at the rear axle. The bus also differed externally, carrying illuminated advertising panels between the decks. The panels were removed during November 1973 when the bus was given an all-over advert for `Busy Bee `, a DIY store, which the bus carried until its withdrawal in 1977. The withdrawal being delayed on account of the all-over advert.

In 1970 LA 284 was the regular bus on an experimental Christmas shoppers` service. Operating between Holland Street and Glasgow Cross, the service ran on a circular route via Sauchiehall Street, Renfield Street, Union Street and Argyle Street before returning via Argyle Street, Hope Street and Bath Street. Despite proving popular with passengers, yet again a Christmas service was to prove a financial flop. Returning to operate only in the afternoons in December 1971, the service still failed to be financially viable and was dropped in 1972.

Scotland's first bus auction took place at Knightswood Garage in September 1978 and LA 284 was included in the buses put under the hammer. Also for sale at the auction were LA 300/12/3/21/3/8/9/35/51/6/62/71. The PTE`s optimism in the potential for further operation of their buses was well founded, as only LA 321 failed to see service again. A second auction of buses was held at Partick Garage in late 1979 with LA 317/9/30/1/7-9/47/ 48/52/7/9/63/8/72/5-9/82/5-7/8/93, although this time a significant proportion of the buses were sold to the Barnsley dealers and saw no further use. The luckier buses were sold to various operators including Allander Coaches, Rapsons of Brora and Ritchies P.S.V. Driving School.

A box shaped LA 269 above, rests between duties for Aberdeen Art Gallery and Museums. When the bus was rebuilt some modern features including a reflective numberplate and large rear view mirrors were added. (A.J.Douglas)

LA 297, in attendance at the Larkfield Garage open day in April 1978, is getting its cab thoroughly tested for its durability by two wee Glasgow boys. Just to their rear is an extra cab window that was inserted to assist the bus in driver training duties. Also visible in this image is the rear of LA 1. (D. Cousins)

LA 285–321

LA 285– 302 DGE 322– 339C Leyland PDR 1/1 Alexander H44/34F
LA 303– 321 GYS 879– 897D Leyland PDR 1/1 Alexander H44/34F
37 buses delivered between September 1965 and September 1966.

Despite Atlantean deliveries having reached LA 284, it would appear that not everyone on the transport committee was convinced as to the merits of the front entrance/ rear engine combination. In a submission to the committee on the 18th August 1965, Mr Fitzpayne quoted from the 'Leeds Transport Report' for the year ending 31st March 1965,

'The introduction into the fleet of modern front entrance double deck motor-buses has proved to be very popular with the travelling public and future orders for new vehicles provide for an increasing number of this type.'

What was not open for discussion was the increased comfort and safety of the front entrance bus. GCT had surveyed boarding and leaving times of passengers at bus stops and discovered that a rear entrance bus took 1.15 seconds per passenger to board as opposed to 1.23 seconds per passenger for the Atlantean. It was believed that the doors on the Atlantean were the reason for the increased boarding time. The doors however helped to keep the saloon warm and more importantly stopped passengers jumping on or off the buses whilst it was moving. In 1962 GCT had carried out a survey of boarding and leaving accidents amongst its fleet of 1289 buses, 311 of which were forward entrance. The results published in 1965 were:-

Boarding and Leaving Accidents 1/1/62— 31/12/62

Type of entrance	Rear	Front
No. of Accidents	1 823	181
Miles Operated	35 326 425	8 211 284
Miles per Accident	19 372	45 366

The Chief Constable of Glasgow Police, J.A. Robertson, wrote to Mr Fitzpayne agreeing with the findings of the survey. Accidents involving a bus, of course, had legal consequences for the Corporation if negligence on their part could be proved. Between April 1961 and November 1962, 38 claims were made against the Corporation which were settled at a cost of £ 1336. Although GCT directives stated that a rear entrance bus should not move until the conductor was on the platform and had signalled to the driver, this caused delay and obstructed other road users if observed. The front entrance half cabs at least allowed the driver to check the platform himself, but it required the driver to turn round and left him without a totally clear view of the platform. The front entrance/ rear engine bus had the added benefit to the driver of having the platform ahead of the front axle, thus giving unobstructed views of the platform from the driver's seat. This was very important if the conductor was otherwise occupied, reducing the risk of the bus pulling away whilst passengers were still boarding. Another small benefit of the rear engine bus was the driver did not have to sit next to the engine during his shift, this coupled with the smoother riding of the more modern bus helped to make the driver's day less tiring.

Essentially just a follow on order from the previous batch, there were no major design alterations. Only LA 320 from this batch stands out. Withdrawn in 1979, the bus was sold to Windsorian Coaches of Windsor who converted the bus to open top and from July 1979, used it for 'Royal Heritage Tours' and evening pub tours around Windsor. The front dash panel was modified by the addition of large square side lights and indicators and the driver's seat was replaced with a sheepskin covered seat. Sold to Guide Friday tours in 1990, LA 320 later operated for its new owners in Windermere, 1990, Plymouth, 1991/2 and Brighton 1993/5. In 2001 the bus was purchased for preservation and returned to Glasgow where it has since been re-roofed with the roof from LA 391 and repainted into GCT livery.

LA 322

LA 322 GYS 898D Leyland PDR 1/1 Alexander H44/34F
1 bus delivered in November 1966.

Prior to entering service LA 322 spent a week at Larkfield Bus Works where it was available for inspection by members of the transport committee. Without doubt an experimental bus, it was fitted with a Voith Diawabus automatic gearbox, which was of German manufacture. Voith gearboxes were already being used by GCT in Leyland Panthers LS 31/2 and a further example would come fitted with LS 33. That LA 322 should be fitted with a Voith gearbox was at the behest of the transport department who during 1966 had decided that a double deck bus should also receive this transmission. Entering service from Newlands Garage in early December 1966, the bus initially made a good impression. After completing 21 000 miles, the drivers were reporting favourably on the bus and GCT was also pleased with satisfactory fuel consumption figures. Unfortunately for Voith GCT would later specify other gearbox systems for its buses and to this end the remaining Panthers, LS 34– 46, were fitted with Self Changing Gears, SCG, transmission.

It wasn't only under the bonnet that LA 322 was experimental. The top deck of the bus was fitted with fibre glass seats and the lower deck had grey/green leather cloth seats. The transport department was particularly proud of how graffiti was less of a problem on LA 322. On 10th December 1966 the bus had its upper rear seat defaced with black ink. After being removed the next day, LA 322 returned to service on the 12th. Had ordinary leatherette been fitted, the graffiti could not have been removed and the bus would have been withdrawn until the leatherette had been replaced.

Melamine was extensively used throughout LA 322 with bodyside panels between waist and side rail as well as a full depth entrance partition receiving this material at a cost of an extra £ 43. The staircase, lower saloon bulkhead and the driver's partition assembly were finished in Melamine faced sheets which added £ 16 to costs and Melamine coated pillar fascias added an extra £ 2.

After a spell at Bridgeton Garage, LA 322 was converted to 'OMO' and returned to Newlands Garage during 1968 to allow it to operate service 21 whenever LA 362 was unavailable. As it aged, LA 322 was delicensed on several occasions as the Voith gearbox began to prove troublesome in later years. In June 1971 the bus was parked up and remained out of use until August 1974 when the PTE, by now desperate for serviceable vehicles, fitted a semi automatic gearbox to the bus.

Despite those three years' inactivity in the early seventies, the bus was withdrawn in 1979 along with other Atlanteans delivered during 1966. LA 322 later found use with Ritchies PSV driving school who bought the bus in April 1979 along with several other ex PTE Atlanteans. After a repaint into a mainly maroon livery with white upper deck windows, the buses were used to help train new drivers for the PTE.

Traversing George Square behind a GGPTE panoramic bodied Atlantean, the former LA 322 undertakes driver training duties for Ritchies Training Centre. The fitting of a LA 501– 600 style front panel to PDR Atlanteans from earlier batches was common as the buses aged and LA 322 was far from unique in this respect. (David G. Wilson)

LA 323–364

LA 323– 364 KUS 578– 619E Leyland PDR 1/1 Alexander H44/34F
42 buses delivered between January and June 1967.

LA 325 became the first Atlantean to be permanently allocated to Langside Garage around June 1968. Prior to this an Atlantean from Larkfield Garage was loaned each night to Langside for operation of night bus service 2. No Atlanteans had been allocated here previously as the internal layout of the garage had been unsuitable for the chassis. Well that is the official reason, unofficially it had more to do with an official within the garage disliking the rear engined bus and successfully using the garage's internal layout as an excuse to keep them out of Langside. Eventually GCT decided to test fit an Atlantean into Langside and surprise, surprise, the bus fitted! Before long the Atlantean ruled the roost at Langside and the garage's allocation of halfcabs were just a memory. To be fair, there was justification for disliking the Atlantean. Regardless of what the sales brochures said, it was a more complicated bus and thus more time consuming to mechanics than the buses it replaced. It also had reliability problems, most notably electrics and overheating engines.

LA 362 joined the fleet in June 1967 and had a `Self Changing Gears` automatic transmission fitted in place of its semi-automatic transmission the next month, although it initially remained in use as a crew operated bus. It was at this time that LA 362 moved from Bridgeton Garage to Newlands with Voith gearbox fitted LA 322 going the opposite way. The German built Voith gearbox added £ 739 12/- to the cost of a Leyland Panther and in an effort to reduce costs, a Leyland automatic unit, £ 250 per chassis, was fitted to LA 362. By the first week of September 1967 the Transport Department reported that LA 362 had covered 4 000 trouble free miles. The SCG unit had several advantages over its German counterpart as no structural changes were needed to the chassis, the SCG box did not add weight to the chassis and the British unit was an electrical operation as opposed to the torque converter in the Voith unit; this meant that there were no overheating problems and consequently a reduction in the strain on the engine cooling system. Not that the engine needed any help in putting strain on the cooling system, it was heroically managing this task on its own.

LA 362 was also the first Atlantean to be converted for OMO and to aid the bus in its new role it was given change trays, ticket machine holder and a periscope to allow the driver a clearer view of the upper saloon. As there would be no conductor to help with reversing, redundant AEC Regent 3 headlamps were fitted at the rear of the bus, under the upper deck overhang. The bus subsequently acquiring the nickname, `Yellow Submarine`. To tell the public that the driver took the fares, the legend, `one man operated bus pay as you enter`, was placed above the entrance. A similar message was also carried on a small black board above the nearside headlight.

At the 1967 Kelvin Hall Show, LA 362 was used as an external demonstrator whilst inside LS 33 was on display. In February 1968, LA 362 went on loan to Western SMT and was tested on the Kilmarnock to Ardrossan service with the bus finally entering one man service with GCT later that month on service 21, Midland Street— Pollok. Its operation would have a significant impact in the decision making process of future OMO vehicle purchases by GCT. Withdrawn in 1978, LA 362 was purchased by Shennan of Drongan in September 1978 and Sykes of Carlton acquired the bus for disposal in November 1981.

Loading in Oswald Street is LA 330. The Bells Whisky advert was synonymous with Glasgow buses for many years. (David. G. Wilson)

LA 365– 421

LA 365– 414 MUS 250– 299F Leyland PDR 1/1 Alexander H44/34F
LA 415– 421 NUS 835– 841F Leyland PDR 1/1 Alexander H44/34F
57 buses delivered between August 1967 and March 1968.

In January 1966, Leyland provided GCT with Park Royal, H74F, bodied Atlantean demonstrator KTD 551C. Operated for a week on service 61, Maryhill– Tollcross, the bus was fitted with the more powerful 0.680 engine instead of the GCT preference for Atlanteans, the 0.600 engine. The Atlantean by its size was a heavier vehicle than earlier Leyland products, for which the 0. 600 engine was fitted, and this was evident with a full load aboard. The 0.680 engine was more powerful and Leyland felt it was better suited to the Atlantean`s operating conditions. Drivers liked the demonstrator as the extra power gave a smoother take off from a standing start and there was less use of the gearbox. The drivers also felt that maintaining schedules on the cross city route was easier and that passengers received less jolting than usual. Interestingly, the fuel consumption for the 0.680 engine was identical to the 0.600 engine. It was felt that the provision of more power in the lower gears would result in less maintenance on units such as the gearbox and carden shafts. KTD 551C also operated on hire to Western SMT and it would be 1992 before Western and GCT`s successor, Strathclyde Buses, were to share another Park Royal bodied Atlantean.

Mr Fitzpayne had notified the transport committee in July 1965 that 100 buses would be needed to replace the trolleybuses and that a further 50 buses would be needed for fleet replacement. When the transport committee met in April 1966 they approved an order for 150 Atlanteans with the more powerful 0.680 engine at an extra cost of £ 45 per chassis. The total cost of the order was £ 1 050 705, which is £ 3 184 per body and £ 3 820 per chassis. This order would later be reduced to 136 Atlanteans, LA 365—500, after a meeting of transport committee in April 1967. The deleted 14 Atlanteans being replaced by a similar number of Leyland Panthers, LS 33– 46. These buses would complement LS 31/2, which were already in service. There may have been good reason for buying saloons, but it would be another 30 years before single deck buses found widespread acceptance in the fleet.

At the start of May 1966, trolleybus route 101 was replaced by a bus service between Riddrie and Rutherglen. Due to alternative services covering the entire length of its route, service 102 , Royston Road– Polmadie, was withdrawn without replacement. The final trolleybus ran on the 27th of May 1967, ending not only 18 years of `the silent death` as Glaswegians knew the trolleys, but 69 years of electric public transport on Glasgow's streets.

This new batch of Atlanteans had air operated pedestal gearchange that was floor mounted instead of the usual electric gearchange, but from 1974 onwards these vehicles were fitted with electric gearchanges during overhaul, as would LA 422– 500. As with LA 284, these buses had a ramped floor in the lower saloon and upstairs sliding windows replaced the hopper windows used previously. The upstairs emergency rear window was now a large single piece of glass in place of the two small windows used until LA 364. In October 1967, LA 383-7 were the first Atlanteans allocated to Gartcraig Garage, with the last garage to receive Atlanteans, Langside, finally getting some LA`s in the summer of 1968. LA 390—421 were fitted with air operated doors and LA 399, which appeared at the 1967 Millburn Motors show, had Luminator interior lighting for advertising panels on both decks.

March 1977 and LA 381 is in Argyle Street with the second version of the Transcard advert that the bus carried from July 1976 until May 1979 when LA 381 was withdrawn. (D. Cousins)

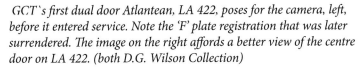

LA 422

PYS 950G Leyland PDR 1/1 Alexander H45/30D
1 bus delivered in July 1968.

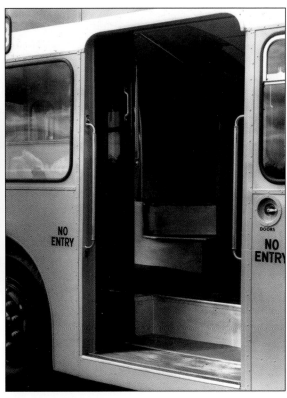

GCT`s first dual door Atlantean, LA 422, poses for the camera, left, before it entered service. Note the 'F' plate registration that was later surrendered. The image on the right affords a better view of the centre door on LA 422. (both D.G. Wilson Collection)

By early 1968 Atlanteans accounted for nearly one third of the GCT fleet of 1305 buses, although the peak vehicle requirement was only 1066. As the number of Atlanteans owned continued to increase, so changes were required to infrastructure to allow operation of the rear engined bus. One example being in Saint Enoch Square, where the stances for services 7 and 12 were moved to the east side of the square from the 3rd of March 1968 to allow for Atlantean operation on these routes.

In June 1968 Mr Fitzpayne reported to the transport committee that an Atlantean had been converted to OMO dual door specification by Alexanders, the first of 287 such Atlanteans for the fleet. This bus, he said, would be made available for inspection by the transport committee. It is interesting to note the additional seat that is added to the upper deck seating capacity; was it to compensate for the loss of four seats downstairs? Mr Fitzpayne also reported that Alexanders could convert 36 Atlanteans due that autumn, LA 423– 458, to dual door specification for an extra £ 447 per body. As it turned out the next dual door Atlanteans would not arrive until August 1969, LA 466 onwards, and in the interim deliveries resorted to the single door variant. However, a new Transport Bill was making its way through Parliament during the summer of 1968 and it was expected to become an act of Parliament that autumn.

A significant part of the Act was that a grant of 25% would be paid towards new buses adapted for one man operation. This obviously had an influence on bus purchases in the UK and effectively killed off the front engine half cab bus, with the last such bus entering UK service during 1970.

At 8 feet 2 1/2 inches wide, LA 422 conformed to the then new maximum width regulations of the time. The bus had a step at the entrance and then a flat floor thereafter in the lower saloon, electrically operated doors and a forward ascending staircase that commenced between the two doors. Although delivered in July 1968, it would be November of that year before LA 422 entered service, by which time the bus had been reregistered PYS 950G. The booked registration of PUS 318F being released, although LA 422 did have publicity photographs taken carrying the 'F' registration plate.

As expected LA 422 entered service from Newlands Garage on service 21 alongside the other OMO buses, but in the autumn of 1969 it was transferred to Possilpark Garage when LA 466 onwards entered service on route 28. In 1975 the bus was rebuilt to H45/29F configuration and LA 422 was withdrawn by GGPTE during 1979. The bus was sold to an English dealer in April 1980 and was last recorded with a Barnsley dealer in December 1980.

LA 423–500

LA 423– 458 PYS 951– 986G Leyland Atlantean PDR 1/1 Alexander H44/34F
LA 459– 464 UGA 212– 217H Leyland Atlantean PDR 1/1 Alexander H44/34F
LA 465– 500 UGA 218– 253H Leyland Atlantean PDR 1/1 Alexander H45/30D
78 buses delivered between August 1968 and May 1970.

LA 423– 464 were the last single door PDR Atlanteans delivered to GCT and were similar to LA 365– 421 delivered the previous year. With the impending arrival of OMO, the dual door Panthers and the limited experience of LA 422, it was no great surprise that LA 465– 500 were to dual door formation. The six months that passed between the arrival of LA 443 in December 1968 and LA 444 in June 1969 were to be significant. In these six months GCT was finally given permission for unrestricted OMO operation and LA 444– 60/2/4 were delivered fitted for OMO. Despite its late arrival, LA 461 would not be converted to OMO until April 1975, LA 464 being notable for having the older, LA 2– 364, style of upper rear emergency door.

LA 465– 500 were 8 feet 2 1/2 inches wide and dual door and, as future deliveries would, came fitted for OMO. Prior to delivery, LA 465 had been used by Alexanders as a mock up of the body the company would fit to Atlanteans destined for Liverpool. This bus, which had an automatic gearbox, Luminator lighting and passenger counter, as did LA 474, also appeared at the 1969 Scottish Motor Show. The passenger counter consisted of two digital displays, one for the driver and the other for the passengers. It told those concerned how many empty seats were available on the top deck. A sensitive step on the staircase registered the number of passengers ascending the stairs, the only drawback was if someone stood twice on the step, this misled the counter. Despite its delivery in January 1970, LA 465 was another bus that remained out of service for several months, not entering service until May 1970.

LA 467/9 were initially used for crew training on the dual doors before entering service from Possilpark Garage in September 1969 on service 28, Renfrew Street —Milton. When GCT decided to introduce the Bell Autoslot ticket system in February 1970, service 28 was chosen for the trial and LA 466– 81 were the buses to be fitted with the new equipment. Following the introduction of LA 322, Mr Fitzpayne had suggested that 50 buses be fitted with fibre glass seats and melamine backing instead of imitation leather. LA 451– 64/66– 500 were all fitted out with fibre glass seats upstairs, although LA 469 was to receive them in both decks. The public were not as keen on the seats as Mr Fitzpayne and seats from withdrawn buses was used to replace the fibre glass seats in at least LA 459/72/3/8/9/80/1.

LA 443, mentioned earlier on this page, was withdrawn with accident damage in June 1978 and LA 490 was sold by the PTE to the National Playbus Association in October 1980 for use as a playbus.

The rear end of LA 480 is seen in the west end in the mid-seventies. Several differences are visible when compared to the image of LA 284 on the rear cover. The one piece upper rear emergency door, revised brake and reversing lights and extra air vents on the bonnet of LA 480 are obvious. (A.J.Douglas)

LA 501–550

LA 501– 508 UGA 254– 261H Leyland Atlantean PDR 1A/1 Alexander H45/30D
LA 509– 550 XGA 7– 48J Leyland Atlantean PDR 1A/1 Alexander H45/30D
50 buses delivered between June 1970 and January 1971.

The transport committee met on the 12th August 1968 to consider tenders for bus chassis, commencing LA 501. The decision was held up pending a decision on whether future OMO buses should be single or double deck. Three companies submitted tenders for the work to supply `chassis with tyres`:-

Leyland Motors	£ 3918 5 0d per chassis
Bristol Commercial Vehicles	£ 4112 6 0d per chassis
Daimler Transport Vehicles	£ 4174 0 6d per chassis

It was fairly clear that the new buses were to be supplied by Leyland, but single or double deck? This issue was to be resolved when the transport committee met again on the 28th of August. Mr Fitzpayne submitted the following points which influenced the committee to continue purchasing double deck buses:-

1. Single deck vehicles would be 36 feet long, whereas a double deck bus is 30 feet long. Single deck buses therefore require more road and depot space.

2. Single deckers carry 73 passengers, a double decker carries 80 passengers. To opt for the former would represent a 9% drop in seats and therefore more buses would be needed.

3. The single decker has 42 seats and 31 standing whereas the double decker has 75 seats and 5 standing.

4. The length of the single decker makes it less manoeuvrable.

5. Since February 1968, a double decker, LA 362, has already satisfactorily operated service 21, Midland Street to Pollok.

On the 29th October 1968, Mr Fitzpayne reported to the transport committee that Alexanders and Park Royal had each submitted bids to body the 150 chassis on order. As Alexanders had submitted the lower bid, this was Mr Fitzpayne`s recommended choice. It had been intended that the buses would start to arrive in 1970 at a rate of 10 vehicles per month. As only 100 PDR Atlanteans were delivered by April 1972, this delivery specification clearly became unsustainable. What became of the other 50 PDR chassis is unclear, there are suggestions that the first 50 AN 68s, LA 601-650, completed this order.

One reason why MCW Metropolitans were ordered in 1972 was the Corporation's displeasure at the way Leyland went about supplying GCT with chassis and spare parts. At the start of 1970 GCT had 57 Atlanteans off the road with gearbox problems whilst engineers waited on Leyland to supply the spare parts. Indeed officials from GCT had talks with the chief executive of Leyland, Arthur Fogg, at the end of January 1970 regarding the delay in supplies of spare parts. GCT were looking for three assurances :-

- an official date when the 57 defective Atlanteans would return to service;
- that supplies of spares would be forthcoming to keep the existing fleet roadworthy;
- that the above problems would not be repeated with the forthcoming order for 150 Atlanteans due to start arriving in February 1970.

Indeed it was made clear to Mr Fogg at this meeting that Glasgow was considering cancelling further orders and would look to foreign chassis suppliers if necessary. Leicester by this time had already taken buses from an European bus manufacturer.

LA 501 introduced a revised front dash with more raised mouldings than the style used previously, the chassis code, PDR 1A/1, reflecting the use of the rationalised pneumo-cyclic gearbox. New features included a spring parking brake, power steering and a return to electric gearchange on the steering column. All these buses came fitted for OMO and had radios,£ 225 extra per bus at October 68 prices. Mr Fitzpayne had commented to the transport committee, `The cost of fitting two way radio is high and will also entail added maintenance costs. It can only be justified as the committee knows because of hooliganism, which is a more serious matter when there is no conductor to assist the driver. Fourteen of our buses are fitted with two way radios and this has been useful in reporting incidents on the bus and also a quick means of reporting mechanical defects on route.` The experiment which was based at Ibrox Garage had begun in April 1968 and used LA 142/5-7/51/62-4/70/336/48/67/8/422. The buses were in direct communication with Head Office in Bath Street where a Duty Inspector was also in touch with mobile patrol vans. Radios were subsequently fitted during 1968 to the still very small OMO fleet where their value was appreciated even more. By 1969 it was decided to spend £ 20 000 fitting radios to a further 100 buses already in service.

On some of these buses the `Leyland – Albion Atlantean` badge was fitted, but the majority had the new style rectangular `ATLANTEAN` badges, silver letters on a black background, which were fitted at the front only. LA 502-50 had Luminator lighting fitted to the interior advertising panels. Rarely if ever used, the biggest contribution Luminator lighting made was in giving the bus a flat battery. In the course of recertification most of the batch had every alternate Luminator panel removed in 1977, although LA 524 had all of its Luminator panels removed in 1974 and replaced by standard lighting. During 1977 revised air intakes were fitted to the batch, these closely resembled the type fitted to AN 68 models.

LA 504 was delivered in August 1970 and within two months the bus had been fitted with a new front dash to the previous design after sustaining serious accident damage.

LA 510 became a motorway maintenance vehicle with Strathclyde Regional Council in August 1981. It was fitted with sliding roof panels that allowed ladders to reach overhead motorway gantries from the upper deck. Now in preservation, the bus is presently in a dilapidated state and will require a lot of work to restore it to original condition. Due to the shortage of GCT PDR Atlanteans in preservation, it is hoped that the bus will survive, although unlikely. However LA 517 is rumoured to still exist in Wales, so perhaps one good bus can be made from two donor vehicles.

LA 521 is notable for having a plastic lower saloon emergency door.

LA 526 was repainted into GGPTE livery and reflective fleetnumber plates for the Omnibus Society Presidential Weekend in June 1974. Despite the earlier failures of Christmas operations, the PTE decided to get in on the act in December 1975 when ` park and ride` service 75 was introduced. Named the CityShopper it ran from the 8th till the 31st December on a route that connected Argyle Street with car parks in the Gorbals. Operating on a six minute frequency from 0900 till 1830, the service was operated by three Larkfield based OMO fitted Atlanteans, from a pool of LA 549/50/9/63/8. Despite a fare of 8 pence for adults and 4 pence for children, once again the service was not a financial success.

LA 507 with large fleetnumbers unloads in the city centre, just above the route number box the exposed aerial for the two way radio is visible. The board advising passengers that the bus was one man operated was fixed in place and was misleading if the bus was allocated to a crew route. Note also that the three vented windows on the offside lower deck were nearest the rear axle on new dual door Atlanteans, new short bay bodied single door examples having their three vented windows nearest the front offside axle. (David. G. Wilson)

LA 551– 600

LA 551– 600 BGA 509– 558K Leyland Atlantean PDR 1A/1 Alexander H45/30D
50 buses delivered between September 1971 and April 1972.

Fourteen years of PDR Atlantean purchases by the Corporation ended with this batch, these buses would also be the last steel framed Atlanteans supplied to Glasgow by Alexanders. By the time the buses arrived, Alexanders had been using alloy framed bodywork for two years. As with the previous batch, Luminator lighting was included and was also removed in the same manner as described for LA 502– 50, the air intakes also being changed at recertification. LA 551- 600 had split windscreens and cab radios fitted, the latter by then becoming quite familiar in the fleet. The aerial was mounted in front of the upper deck windscreen, which unfortunately made the aerials vulnerable to mechanical bus washes at garages.

LA 553 was the last PDR Atlantean to operate in service with PTE when it was withdrawn on the 12th of May 1981.

Three months later the bus was purchased for preservation, but unfortunately it was discovered that the bus was not suitable for preservation and soon passed to Tiger, dealer of Salsburgh in Lanarkshire.

LA 574 was exhibited at the 1971 Scottish Motor Show with features that included a recessed fluorescent cab light and an anti—vandal alarm. This latter piece of equipment later became standard and could be activated by passengers or crew. Upon activation a klaxon would sound and it was hoped that anyone hearing this would dial 999 for the police. The cost of fitting the klaxons to the fleet was £ 36 000.

LA 599 and LA 600 came fitted with automatic gearboxes. A Lucas CAV unit was fitted in LA 599 and a Self Changing Gears unit was fitted in LA 600.

LA 597 may still have carried GCT livery, but the bus was part of the GGPTE fleet when it was photographed in George Square. It is interesting to note that the legal lettering on the bus has been relocated due to the centre door. The dilapidated building to the rear of LA 597 has since been replaced by the modern design of George House, the Glasgow offices of Ernst and Young. (A. J Douglas).

LA 601– 750

LA 601– 650 FUS 121– 170L Leyland AN68/1R Alexander H45/30D
LA 651– 710 HGD 857– 916L Leyland AN68/1R Alexander H45/30D
LA 711– 750 NGB 79– 118M Leyland AN68/1R Alexander H45/30D
150 buses delivered between November 1972 and December 1973

Without doubt one of the most exciting periods for Atlantean deliveries to GCT or any of it's successors, LA 601– 750 would have the last short bay bodies until LA 1351 arrived in August 1980. The chassis for these buses was the then new AN 68/1R, the `68` relating to the now standard 0.680 engine and the `R` related to the steering being right hand drive. The new chassis was not that different from the previous PDR chassis, the layout was basically the same and a weakness from the previous design which was included were the radiator mountings on the chassis. The mountings supported not only the radiator, but also the gearbox and angle drive which led to the support bracket breaking. Some operators would weld the broken bracket, but this wasn't a long term solution as the repair would eventually break again. When working on the problem of the defective PDR Atlanteans, Chief Engineer Alan Westwell had found that if the engines were idling at lower than the correct speed, they would produce vibrations as the engine hunted. These vibrations manifested themselves in strains on the radiator and its mounting. He therefore ensured that engine idling speeds were correct and he also modified the design of the radiator mounting bracket which helped to overcome the problem in the longer term. Other changes that Leyland introduced were the chassis frame being redesigned to allow

a 4 feet 4 1/4 inch front entrance and the rear overhang was lengthened to allow back to back seating over the rear axle. To protect the steering box and brake controls from accident damage, the front chassis crossmember was moved forward. To lessen bodywork damage when the bus was under tow, the towing faces were also moved forward. The engine area was also subject to some redesigning with the engine covers altered for easier access. The three piece engine cover had a counter balanced, self supporting centre section with the end panels vertically hinged and given revised air intakes. A shield was fitted around the engine to stop dirt reaching the drive belts and propeller shaft. The biggest change to the engine was the addition of a fully charged fluid coupling which used the same oil as the angle drive and gearbox and which led to considerable cooling of all three components. The engine's cooling systems were also modified; a larger capacity radiator header tank was fitted as was a redesigned water pump, which gave increased flow through the engine block. Radalarm, a warning system that gave visual and audible warnings to the driver that engine coolant was falling below safe levels was a new addition. Power steering and a duplicate starter switch under the bonnet were also incorporated into the bus.

LA 601– 750 introduced the Alexander 'AL' body to the

LA 642 heads down Victoria Road close to Larkfield Garage. Compare this bus to LA 687 on the front cover and the different windscreen wiper recesses and indicators used on both buses are apparent. (David.G.Wilson)

fleet; this was really just a flatter version of the body used until LA 600. The roof was flattened and the windows on both decks were now of equal depth, but the biggest change was to the body structure. Alloy framed bodywork, around which the body was constructed, was introduced to the fleet with LA 601, replacing the previous all steel body frame. White and yellow registration plates were used for the first time, replacing the black and white style of registration plate used previously. With the Greater Glasgow Passenger Transport Executive, GGPTE, assuming control of the bus fleet on the 1st of June 1973 from GCT, the fleet got a new manager.

Ronald Cox was the first Director General of the PTE and came to the job form Edinburgh, where he had been its Transport Manager since 1964. Previous to this he had spent two years as the Transport Manager at Bournemouth. The seventh and last GCT Transport Manager was William Murray who became Director of Operations with the PTE. The GCT livery was altered slightly with the arrival of LA 601, wheels now being painted Brunswick green and bumpers painted black. These were subsequently fitted retrospectively to previous deliveries. Most of the 150 buses had one piece windscreens when new, however, LA 614/5/8-20/634-45/712-50 had split windscreens. In an attempt to defeat vandalism LA 604 had the thirteen rearmost seats in the upperdeck changed to fibreglass in the summer of 1977. LA 644, new to Langside Garage, had its body destroyed by fire in July 1973 and emerged from Alexanders at Falkirk in February 1974 with a new panoramic body which had been intended for LA 793. During the month, the bus returned to service from Langside. When LA 644 was delicensed, LA 621 was transferred from Newlands Garage to Langside as a replacement. As Newlands was receiving

new Atlanteans around the LA 700 mark at the time, it is possible this transfer was to maintain the age profile of the fleet at Langside.

LA 664 was the longest serving Atlantean in the fleet. New in April 1973 to Gartcraig Garage in GCT livery it lasted until 1997 by which time it had reacquired GCT livery. To emphasise LA 664`s longevity it is worth noting that LA 663 was withdrawn in March 1983 and LA 665 was withdrawn in May 1983 although LA 664 was listed as withdrawn for a while during 1985. LA 663 was rumoured to be in preservation in 1997, but by 2000 the bus had been scrapped. LA 663/5 were both converted to single door during 1977, but it would be another two years before LA 664 was similarly converted. By September 1989 LA 664 was the oldest bus in the SBL fleet and as part of the Centenary of Public Transport celebrations, the bus was repainted into GCT livery in 1994, although the bus was delivered in dual door format. It was at this time that the bus was transferred from SBL to the Comlaw GCT fleet and although supposed to be operating service 100, SECC and City Centre, the bus could often be seen operating school services in Milngavie. Possibly because it was the last GCT bus left in the service fleet, LA 664 had a bit of status attached to it. For a long time it was the only Atlantean without engine shrouds in passenger service, although this changed with the second-hand buses bought after the Larkfield fire in May 1992. Unfortunately its status was not able to save the bus from the scrapyard and LA 664 was dispatched to Wigley of Carlton in the spring of 1998.

The last buses delivered to GCT, LA 690– 5 were also the first buses licensed by GGPTE, LA 695 being the last new GCT bus. A new feature on these buses were engine shrouds which had been added at the request of Mr Cox.

LA 644, complete with a new panoramic bodywork, takes it`s layover in Saint Enoch. (David. G Wilson).

Giving the buses a distinctly Edinburgh appearance, it is worth noting that all three fleets that Mr Cox had control over bought buses adorned with engine shrouds. It follows that LA 696 was the first new bus delivered to the PTE, still carrying GCT livery and legal lettering , the bus even had the name of the last GCT General Manager, William Murray, on it. Indeed deliveries of GCT liveried Atlanteans continued until LA 716. Although all of the LA 696– 716 batch were quickly repainted into GGPTE livery, without GG logos, some buses were put to work in GCT livery.

LA 697 was new to Newlands Garage on the 1st July 1973. Prior to this the bus had been involved in livery trials at the Bus Works. In later life the bus worked from the driving school and is presently in the hands of preservationists in the Glasgow area. Last seen at the Glasgow Bus Museum open day in 2001 converted back to its original dual door specification, the bus carried an all white livery. For a while it appeared this would be the first bus preserved in GGPTE livery, but sadly it is yet to be finished in GGPTE livery. Indeed by late 2004 it was languishing inside Larkfield Garage and was donating parts to keep First Glasgow's Atlantean tour fleet on the road. LA 907 has since become the first preserved bus to wear GGPTE livery.

LA 710 was converted to single door form in 1978 and given a LA 751 type destination display in June 1980. This last feature was removed when the bus was converted to a driver trainer in September 1983. It was at this time the bus was also converted to H—/—C specification with an outward opening hinged door.

Whilst operating service 45 to Carnwadric on the 15th March 1976, LA 733 suffered serious fire damage at the hands of vandals during the evening rush hour. The bus which had been new to Possilpark Garage on the 1st of July 1973, suffered an estimated £ 8 500 worth of damage, most of which was to the rear of the front axle. Unlike LA 644, the bus was rebuilt at the Bus Works and returned to service with its centre doors removed and to H45/29F formation. No one was hurt in the incident and for this the driver must take credit. After being alerted to the upstairs fire by a passenger he went upstairs to investigate and was quoted as saying, 'When I went upstairs I found most of the passengers just sitting watching. It seemed to be getting worse by the second and one man had his head out of the window because he could not breathe for the fumes. I had no hesitation in getting everyone off the bus'. One passenger later said, 'I felt my seat getting hot and when I turned around there was a lot of smoke. When I got up I found several lighted sheets of newspaper under my seat.'

In June 1974 LA 739 became Scotland's first transport recruitment bus. Despite a 22% increase in staff recruitment in 1973/4 over 1972/3, staff wastage was running at 52%. The bus was converted into an exhibition area downstairs and had recruiting offices upstairs. Decorated with recruiting slogans, it was planned that the bus would appear at shows, carnivals, processions and exhibitions. LA 739 was subsequently modified to single door layout and returned to service with a revised recruiting livery.

LA 706, wearing the second PTE livery, turns from Bath Street into Renfield Street in June 1981. Despite being only eight years old, the bus was already wearing its third version of fleet livery. Interestingly, this bus has a fleetnumber plate on the front panel, yet GCT silver transfers for the fleetnumber above the offside front axle. (David.G. Wilson)

LA 751– 825

LA 751– 760 NGB 119– 128M Leyland AN68/1R Alexander H45/31F
LA 761– 810 OYS 158– 207M Leyland AN68/1R Alexander H45/31F
LA 811– 825 RGB 592– 606M Leyland AN68/1R Alexander H45/31F
75 buses delivered between December 1973 and June 1974

A new batch and yet another variant of the Alexander bodywork was used. Alexander `AL` style bodywork was retained, but this time panoramic windows were fitted to the buses instead of the previously standard short bay style. Until this time the panoramic style of body was associated with Edinburgh buses, whence Mr Cox had come, and independent operators like A1 Service of Kilmarnock and Mc Gills of Barrhead. All of these companies had taken dual door bodies, but the PTE however, and surprisingly considering Mr Cox's Edinburgh connections, ordered single door buses.

LA 751, which had an automatic gearbox, was displayed at the 1973 Scottish Motor Show in the Kelvin Hall. Inside the bus had Edinburgh style lights, a foot pedal for operating the doors, a nearside luggage rack, light green interior and green seats. The destination layout had also been moved with the destination box now on the offside of the bus and the service number parallel, but in its own box , on the nearside. The previous style of display, with the service number above the destination had been used since 1957. The number blinds on the nearside above the front axle continued in use. Resplendent in the new GGPTE livery, the bus introduced the `GG` symbol to the public as well as white fleetnumber plates on the front and both sides of the bus with a yellow fleetnumber plate on the rear engine shroud. Prior to this, black fleetnumber plates with silver digits had been applied to early repaints into PTE livery.

On the 28th February 1974, LA 751 and four staff travelled from Glasgow to Hamburg in Germany to take part in a `Glasgow Week,` earning the bus the nickname, `The Flying Hamburger.` The bus took with it models of the city's future railway systems as well as crates of beer. Adorned with a coat of varnish, wheel rings and a `GB` plate the bus must have looked very smart. Between the decks was a Glasgow Coat of Arms and the message` Grusse aus Schottland von den Glasgower Burgen an die Hamburger Burger` which translates as ` Greetings from the citizens of Glasgow, Scotland to the citizens of Hamburg`. The `Please Pay Driver` sign was changed to read ` Kostenlose Rundfahrten` meaning ` costless round trips.` The bus's height, 14 feet 6 inches, meant that there were frequent difficulties with headroom clearance in Hamburg, but even so, the trip was reported to be an

March 1977 and LA 774 travels southbound through the city centre, its journey having started in Ruchill and proceeded via Byres Road and Charing Cross. The flat roof profile of the post LA 601 Atlanteans is visible in comparing LA 774 to the earlier delivered PDR Atlantean following behind. (D. Cousins)

outstanding success. Whilst in Hamburg LA 751 carried over 7 000 people on short circular trips of the city, with passengers receiving tourist promotional literature of Glasgow.

LA 752– 800 returned to the style of interior used before LA 751 and it would be LA 801 before the `LA 751` style of interior returned, although with standard Glasgow interior lights. LA 752– 798 initially had GCT silver transfers for fleetnumbers, this type of fleetnumber having been used since the city's first motor-buses. The `LA 751` fleetnumber plate would return to use from LA 799 onwards and LA 651 upwards, as well as some older buses, which were subsequently retrofitted with the new style plates.

As noted with LA 751, the `Please Pay Driver` boards were positioned in the top nearside of the windscreen. Lit from the destination box, it could be changed to show `Please Pay Conductor` when required. Once all routes had been converted to OMO the boards were removed. When new LA 751– 800 had only one offside sliding window vent on the lower deck, this was later changed to two window

vents and became standard on later deliveries.

LA 806 had a `G2` automatic transmission when new and this was evaluated on the heavily used routes to Castlemilk, but in April 1978 the unit was replaced by a semi automatic gearbox.

LA 821 , new to Larkfield Garage in July 1974, was stolen in the autumn of that year by a 20 year old conductor who was under the influence of alcohol. The bus crashed into an old folks home causing £ 20 000 worth of damage to the property and £ 3 500 damage to LA 821. Fortunately no one was injured in the accident and the conductor was later to receive nine months at `Her Majesty's` pleasure for his troubles. The bus was repaired and back in service by January 1975. By June 1977 the bus had between decks publicity for centre circle services 77/88, even though the bus was used on a variety of routes from Larkfield Garage. The 77/88 services having been transferred there after the closure of Partick Garage in 1977. LA 821 was later sold to Ulsterbus for spares and gained a fleetnumber despite seeing no passenger service in Ulster.

LA 814, above, is seen in Union Street carrying PTE 2 livery. Despite a large cull of early panoramic bodied Atlanteans in the early eighties, LA 814 survived into the post deregulation Strathclyde Buses fleet. The bus was disposed of to a Glasgow dealer, Blythswood, in the summer of 1988. (David G. Wilson)

LA 826– 850

LA 826– 850 SGA 709– 733N Leyland AN68/1R Alexander H45/31F
25 buses delivered between December 1973 and June 1974

A batch which can only be noted for its mediocrity, as far as I can ascertain only two facts of interest can be attributed to these buses. The first is that when LA 829 entered service it became the highest numbered bus in the fleet. Under the old style numbering scheme the fleetnumbers 827/8 had been given to a pair of Leyland TD 7s , DGB 442/3, that had been new in 1942. The second fact relates to LA 850, new to Ibrox Garage, which was rebuilt as single decker SA 1 in 1982. LA 850 carried an all over advert for `Carlsberg Lager` from November 1975 until May 1978 and later carried an all over advert for `Stakis Hotels` from April 1986 until May 1987.

LA 843 saw further use after the PTE with Ayrshire operator Smith of Patna. The bus was withdrawn by the company after breaking down with gearbox trouble on a trip to Kilmarnock several years ago and until recently it resided in the yard of Smith of Patna. Despite the gearbox, the engine was apparently okay and until recently the bus was complete with a Newlands Garage destination screen, which has now been removed, When seen by the author in October 2004 the bus displayed signs of weathering from having lain out of use for a while, but had a good selection of seats inside. At some point the interior laminate has been painted red and with the lack of early PTE Atlanteans in preservation, LA 843 was amongst the last to have the gear selector on the left of the steering column; this would have made a suitable project for someone with the time, energy and a reasonable amount of money in their hands. However in late 2005, the death knell for the bus was signed when it was purchased to provide spare parts to aid the preservation of both LA 927 and LA 1324.

In the upper picture, a withdrawn LA 843 languishes in the yard of Smith's of Patna in November 2005. (Author)

In the lower picture, LA 850 traverses Jamaica Street in April 1978. When compared to the previous batch, these buses had both windscreen wipers powered from below the windscreen. The bar down the front of the upper windscreen on LA 850 is to protect the radio aerial from the mechanical bus wash and was not as myth has implied, to do with repairing defective panoramic bodies. (D. Cousins)

LA 851– 1050

LA 851– 867 GGG 303– 319N Leyland AN68/1R Alexander H45/31F
LA 868– 892 GNS 660– 684N Leyland AN68/1R Alexander H45/31F
LA 893– 900 HGG 242– 249N Leyland AN68/1R Alexander H45/31F
LA 901– 925 JGA 183– 207N Leyland AN68/1R Alexander H45/31F
LA 926– 950 JUS 773– 797N Leyland AN68/1R Alexander H45/31F
LA 951– 965 KSU 827– 841P Leyland AN68/1R Alexander H45/31F
LA 966– 1000 KSU 842– 876P Leyland AN68A/1R Alexander H45/31F
LA 1001–1050 MDS 664– 713P Leyland AN68A/1R Alexander H45/31F

200 buses delivered between November 1974 and June 1976.

LA 870 is seen in Renfrew Street in May 1975 on a route operated by Knightswood Garage. Note the `Please Pay Driver` sign on the upper nearside of the windscreen. The elderly looking Leyland Titan to the rear, which was new in 1961, belongs to Alexander (Midland) and is travelling to Milngavie. (David.G.Wilson)

By May 1975 the fleet had 1302 buses, of which all bar 16 saloons, were double deckers. Out of this total the PTE had 920 Atlanteans, which at the time made it the largest Atlantean fleet in the world. The withdrawn fleet was also big; there were 106 deckers as well as nine of the saloons awaiting disposal. A mixture of chassis types characterised the remaining operational half cabs, some of which were 17 years old, but their days were now numbered as the PTE was in touch with manufacturers amid hopes of an average fleet age of 12 years in the near future. Admittedly withdrawals, service cuts and garage closures would help in this aim. Bridgeton Garage closed on the 2nd of May 1976 and by April 1977 scheduled mileage had fallen by 5%, but the capacity of the new buses also had to be considered. With 76 seats, the new Atlanteans had larger capacities than the vehicles they were replacing; the rear entrance half cabs had as few as 61 seats and the front entrance half cabs seated 72. Naturally this meant less AN68s were required

to be bought to provide the same number of seats. Even so by May 1977 10.5% of the fleet remained over 13 years old although the average age of the fleet had dropped below seven years old. This latter figure being made possible by the conversion to OMO of over 70% of the scheduled mileage. The 508 buses, mostly Atlanteans, bought between November 1972 and June 1976, show the impact on the age profile of the push to OMO. Evidence of the lowering fleet age could be seen in the virtual cessation of fleet overhauls of the 0.600 engined Atlanteans; instead newer buses were being given early overhauls. A few 1962/3 buses were overhauled, LA 93/104/18/41 for example, but they were given four year instead of seven year Certificates of Fitness. With only LA 93/118 lasting until 1978, few early PDRs came close to expiring their new certificates.

LA 881 was fitted from new with a one piece destination unit to the same design as used on LA 1311– 50 but with the destination box and numberblinds in the same position as all the other Atlanteans from LA 751– 1310. Accident damage saw the bus was fitted with a standard GGPTE destination unit in January 1979.

LA 886– 895 and LA 906– 15 all had automatic gearboxes when new, although semi automatic units were fitted later in their careers. The latter buses having Lucas CAV transmission as well as the right hand gearchange, which had been introduced with LA 901. Prior to this only LA 751 had the gear selector on the offside.

LA 887 had the shortest life of any Atlantean in the fleet, just over three years service. The bus being withdrawn with accident damage during 1978 and disposed to a Barnsley scrapyard in October 1979.

LA 903 was deroofed in May 1979 by the 12 feet 6 inch high Cook Street bridge in the Tradeston area. Whilst undertaking training duties, the inspector had turned to talk with two trainees in the saloon. Unfortunately, the unattended driver had taken a wrong turning which resulted in the bus being crunched. In an indication of the shortage of drivers at the time, the Executive in response to inquiries said, ` It is most likely that the driver will resume training tomorrow, possibly with the same inspector`. After repair the bus returned to service before being withdrawn in 1981. By late 1983, the bus was with Vale of Llangollen Tours in Wales.

LA 907/27 were amongst the last Glasgow Atlanteans to still be in regular service when they were withdrawn in July 2005, the buses having been with Essex operator, Dons of Dunmow since March 1984 and May 1983 respectively. Two other ex GGPTE Atlanteans were also owned, a GNSxxxN example and until recently LA 974 although this has since gone to the great bus garage in the sky!

LA 917 became a playbus for ` Save the Children` and was handed over in December 1983 to the charity's president, Princess Anne, by staff from the Argyle Street store of Marks and Spencer. With its new owner the bus became known as ` Sparky Dragon Bus` and after leaving the charity, it spent from 1998 until 2002 unused in a shed at Knightswood Garage. The bus has been bought by preservationists, but with a big hole at the rear and also a LPG tank over the offside front axle, it is going to require a lot of work if it is to return to the condition of its glory years. Indeed the most recent suggestion for the bus was for it to remain a children's playbus within the Bus World Museum.

Over the years both new and mid-age vehicles have been parked up for various reasons, even when older buses were being returned to service, and LA 938 is one such bus. Damaged as a result of a thunderstorm in August 1975, the bus lay out of use until November 1976 when major repairs were undertaken to return the bus to service.

LA 944/5 had large `Young's` hopper window vents in place of the usual sliding window vents. The `Young's` vent was popular on standard National Bus Company Atlanteans which had Park Royal bodywork and this style of hopper would reappear on Glasgow Atlanteans from LA 1101 onwards.

After being involved in a low bridge accident in 1977, LA 957 was converted to open top configuration and made its debut in the City Tour fleet in 1978. The bus which was also available for private hire survived until November 1988 when Bus and Coach, a dealer from Whitburn, bought it as little more than a shell and soon scrapped it.

In early 1975 Bill Kirkland was appointed Chief Engineer with GGPTE in succession to Alan Westwell, who had left to run the Tayside fleet. Mr Kirkland had been Works and Garages General Manager at Greater Manchester Transport, which was another large Atlantean fleet. The new man preferred the advantages that a single sourced fleet brought and from LA 966 onwards Greater Manchester style control boxes were fitted in the Atlanteans. These vehicles which were chassis code, AN68A/1R, had the rationalised gearbox as well as five speed Leyland National type semi automatic gearchange. Deliveries prior to this had the four speed gearbox.

LA 963 was another bus to be used by Guide Friday as an open topper. The bus underwent a radical metamorphose with its new owner. Besides losing it's roof the bus also lost its engine shrouds and gained a flat front panel, (not of Alexander's making), below the windscreen. LA 963 was used at Windermere in 1990 along with LA 320. The bus later found use at Portsmouth from 1991 to 93 and in Brighton for the 1995 season before returning to Glasgow to operate the company's Glasgow tour for a short time in the summer of 1996.

LA 975 was converted to a survey bus and fitted with office space, toilet facilities, as well as a unique yellow with green skirt livery in 1982 to replace AEC Regent A 350. The AEC, incidentally, survives in preservation in the Glasgow area. By 1985 LA 975 was being used as an exhibition bus in standard orange and black livery. This was to be the last bus owned by SPTE when it was withdrawn in 1988. When the bus fleet had been reorganised in 1986, this bus had not been included in the transfer and subsequently was based at the Executive's Govan premises, i.e. the Underground Depot. The bus was later sold to Blue Bus of Horwich, who at the time had a habit of buying buses from Scottish operators and also saw service with ABC Travel of Formby. Once south of the border, the bus was reseated with moquette seating!

September 1975 would see the chassis of LA 1000 delivered to Alexanders at Falkirk for bodying. It was planned that Lord Stokes, the British Leyland Chairman, would unveil a plaque celebrating the delivery of Glasgow's 1000th Atlantean at the 1975 Scottish Motor Show. By early November things were not going to plan, the bodying of LA 1000 was behind schedule and would not be finished in time for the Motor Show. A few weeks prior to the Show LA 987, KSU 863P, was delivered to Partick Garage and immediately put into store until the Show. When the Show opened LA 987 was displayed to the public as LA 1000 and officially handed over from Lord Stokes to Mr Cox on November 11th. A commemorative plaque was attached to the bus, although this would be removed shortly afterwards. Outside the hall, LA 1 was put on display to allow visitors to make comparisons between the two buses. A shuttle service from the Kelvin Hall to Anderston was also provided and used Atlanteans from the LA 980– 90 batch, minus LA 987 of course. LA 987 was officially renumbered LA 1000 in January 1976 and as far as can be ascertained, the bus never ran as LA 987. The bus saw use at Larkfield Garage and was used in the 1976 City Tour programme. In December 1975 the real LA 1000, KSU 876P, was delivered and put to work as LA 1000. In January 1976 this bus was also renumbered, this time to LA 987, and allocated to Ibrox Garage. This was the first time since 1953 that an unmodified bus had been renumbered in the bus fleet. In 1953 trolleybus TB 35 had been renumbered TBS 1. As if this is not confusing enough, it transpires that an Atlantean from the LA 96x batch was used for publicity photos carrying fleetnumber LA 1000. Despite being withdrawn in the eighties, the real LA 987,KSU 863P, was still active with East Yorkshire, via London Country, until February 1992, whilst the real LA 1000, KSU 876P, eventually found its way to Trurorian of Truro and gave service until 1996.

LA 1000 saw frequent use during the summer of 1977 operating service 99 from Buchannan Bus Station to Anderston Quay. The service was operated in conjunction with the pleasure boats `Queen Mary` and `The Waverley`. The latter ship is said to be the world's last sea going paddle steamer and has recently returned to service after an overhaul. During the summer The Waverley is still popular with Glaswegians -oot fur a day doon the watter- to places like Ayr, Campbletown, The Kyles of Bute and Tignabruich.

LA 1012 was disposed of in December 1980 as a result of fire damage.

LA 1021 `lost the heid` in June 1977 whilst operating the underground replacement service. Despite the presence of route indicators, the driver failed to see them and after a wrong turn he hit the low railway bridge in West Street. This bridge, which is as infamous for bus and lorry strikes

as the bridge in Cook Street, has now been closed off. It remains beyond comprehension how when a driver of a high sided vehicle strikes a multiple strike bridge, all the authorities come down like a ton of bricks on the driver! It is easy to blame the driver, and in some cases the driver is wholly blameworthy, but no one gets out of bed in the morning thinking,` I'll drive into a low bridge today`. Surely those in authority who know only too well of an existing hazard within their jurisdiction should be doing more to have these obstacles removed or altered so they no longer remain a potentially fatal hazard to the public.

LA 1028 which had demister motors experimentally fitted above, instead of below, the windscreen had non-standard vents on either side of the destination display. I remember seeing this bus only once as a wee boy, 9 or 10 years old, in Maryhill Road on the 61 route to Tollcross. Even at such a young age I knew this bus was different. Sold via Lonsdale, dealer of Morecombe to Eastville Coaches of Bristol in August 1983, the bus moved around the independent sector. Most recently with Welsh operator Jones, Bontnewydd t/a Express Motors, the bus was reported as having been bought by a Glasgow preservationist in July 2002. Unfortunately it apparently broke down on its return journey to Glasgow and is said to be in the Manchester area at present.

LA 1042 was withdrawn in 1984 and saw use as a playbus with the ` Gaelic Play Group Association.` The conversion work was undertaken at Larkfield Bus Works and when last heard of, the bus was believed to be in the hands of the Edinburgh Transport Group. This is probably the bus seen from the railway near to Haymarket Station in Edinburgh.

LA 1022, above , was one of three Atlanteans, LA 1000 and LA 1030 being the others, to be used on the 1976 City Bus Tour. LA 1022 received an allover white livery with the others getting yellow and green respectively. (David G. Wilson)

LA 1051– 1250

LA 1051– 1100 RUS 302– 351R Leyland AN68A/1R Alexander H45/31F
LA 1101– 1120 TGE 820– 839R Leyland AN68A/1R Alexander H45/31F
LA 1121– 1150 TGG 736– 765R Leyland AN68A/1R Alexander H45/31F
LA 1151– 1185 UGG 370– 404R Leyland AN68A/1R Alexander H45/33F
LA 1186– 1188 WUS 579– 581S Leyland AN68A/1R Alexander H45/33F
LA 1189– 1200 WUS 567– 578S Leyland AN68A/1R Alexander H45/33F
LA 1201– 1250 XUS 572– 621S Leyland AN68A/1R Alexander H45/33F

200 buses delivered between August 1976 and June 1978.

As early as January 1975 fleetnumbers LA 1051– 1250 had been earmarked for future Atlantean deliveries. With the MCW Metropolitans just starting to appear in service and the Ailsa Volvos still to enter service, it illustrates the task these chassis would have to try and persuade the PTE to stop buying Atlanteans, whatever their shortcomings.

An 8% drop in passengers led to further attempts to reduce costs and Partick Garage shut on April 24th 1977 with the consequent redistribution of services to other garages and a reduction in frequencies. By 1978 the PVR, peak vehicle requirement, would be down to 744 buses from the previous years requirement of 822, the fleet total being down to 1039. Surplus vehicles were withdrawn and in justification of the decision to stop overhauling 0.600 engined Atlanteans in 1975, there would be no buses over 13 years of age in the fleet by April 1978.

LA 1068/94 were fitted with short bays in the lower saloons of their panoramic bodywork to strengthen their bodies between late 1987 and early 1988. LA 1116 would be similarly treated in 1990, and LA 1151 had its lower deck treated in May 1988. LA 1116 was subsequently destroyed in the Larkfield Fire in May 1992.

LA 1083 was one bus to be fitted from new with protruding fog lamps although these were soon removed. As a result of the Larkfield Fire in 1992, several ex Tyne and Wear Atlanteans, fitted with protruding fog lamps, joined the fleet .

LA 1090 and above had `Portovac` windscreen wipers which were positioned above rather than below the windscreen, as had been the case on previous batches. LA 1101 onwards had hopper windows fitted and internally `Cronapress` bell fittings replaced the pull chords which were used by conductors and passengers to alert the driver of the need to stop. LA 1101 was to become GLA 50 in the GCT fleet towards the end of its life, the bus being withdrawn in 1996 after sustaining accident damage.

The lack of public support for the Centre Circle services, 77/88, can be ascertained by an empty LA 1071 in North Hanover Street in March 1977. When photographed the route was still operated by a then doomed Partick Garage. (D. Cousins)

LA 1111 was fitted with an Ailsa `R` type destination screen in August 1986. At the time it was thought that further conversions would follow, however LA 1111 remained unique until its demise in the Larkfield Fire. As a batch of buses, LA 1111– 20 were incredibly unlucky. Besides LA 1111, four other Atlanteans were involved in serious accidents. LA 1115 and LA 1119 were both withdrawn in 1982 after being involved in separate crashes. LA 1117 became SA 6 after hitting a bridge in the summer of 1983. LA 1118 lived long enough to become GLA 47 with GCT before it succumbed to accident damage during 1996. The railway bridge in Cook Street also laid claim to LA 1123 in August 1987, although the bus returned to the front line several months later.

The fold down front made its first appearance on LA 1140/51– 75, the change was made to allow faster electrical repairs to be carried out and would be used again on later delivered LA 1311– 1449. The majority of the buses in this batch subsequently gained standard front dash panels as time went by however. LA 1151 onwards also saw the introduction of back to back seating over the rear axle. As well as being safer than the side seats they replaced, they also increased the lower saloon capacity by two seats. LA 1151– 1200 had been expected before the end of July 1977 as UGG 370– 419R. However, a strike at Alexanders in July and August that year led to the final 15 buses being delayed. The buses finally arrived between August and October, by which time `S` registrations had been acquired for them.

A strange withdrawal was that of LA 1171 after just five years service with the PTE. Presumably withdrawn for mechanical reasons, the bus was sold into independent hands and was still running in October 1988 when Skill of Nottingham sold it to Moffat and Williamson of Gauldry. Its new owner put it to work on local service work in Fife. The last report of this bus was in 1994 when it was sold

to Aberdeenshire operator Burns of Tarves. LA 1187 in 1981 and LA 1188 in 1986, both fire victims, were more mundane withdrawals by comparison.

LA 1193 had found its way to Mc Colls of Dalmuir when it collided with railway bridge at Dumbarton Central Station in May 1990. The bus was deroofed and subsequently withdrawn without repair. Fortunately casualties were light as the bus was nearly empty and only two pensioners were treated for shock following the collision. Mc Colls bought several panoramic bodied Atlanteans from the PTE. However, the company wasn't too impressed with the buses, the PTE having sold the buses for further use without having undertaken structural repairs on their defective bodies. LA 1193 wasn't the only Atlantean to hit this bridge. In September 1988 an unidentified Strathclyde Buses Atlantean was totally deroofed and even made it onto the evening edition of BBC Scotland's Reporting Scotland news bulletin. The bus was shown being driven around one of the company's garages in an open top condition. LA 1416 is also understood to have hit this bridge, although damage was limited to the first upstairs window as the bus didn't go completely under the bridge. Over the years a number of buses have hit this bridge, and still do, due to there being two road bridges under the railway line around 100 yards apart. The bridge right at the station is too low for double deck buses, however the bridge in the Bonhill Road that leads into Strathleven Place is suitable for high sided vehicles.

LA 1204 saw use with GCT but retaining SBL livery after being transferred from the main fleet. In 1997 the bus was sold to Glasgow City Council who repainted the bus in a vivid shade of yellow and applied yellow vinyls across all the windows bar the windscreen, the message ` be fit for life` also being applied to the sides of the bus. Internally, the seats were removed and the bus divided into

A decapitated LA 1117, wearing the third stage PTE livery, poses for the camera inside Larkfield Garage. The force of the impact that the bus took can be gauged by the bent poles on the upper deck . (David.G. Wilson)

small compartments. Towards the end of its career with the council the bus was used as part of the road awareness and safety programme. When the author visited the bus in May 2002 the bus was based at the Polmadie Cleansing Depot in Glasgow and was still roadworthy on account of being serviced every eight weeks. As the bus was too tall for the workshops at Polmadie, the servicing was carried out by an outside contractor. In November 2002 the bus was moved to the Glasgow Bus Museum which was based at the old Bridgeton Garage. This organisation has since become the Glasgow Vintage Vehicle Trust. At present time there are no plans to return the bus to its original condition, although work has been undertaken on the bus and in September 2004, LA 1204 gained a new MoT certificate.

LA 1218 starred in the film ` Carla's Song` that was shot around Glasgow and set in 1987. The film was about a Glasgow bus driver, played by Robert Carlyle, who meets a Nicaraguan refugee. Credit must go the actor for undergoing six days of training with SBL prior to passing his PSV test. The bus itself had all reference to Strathclyde Buses covered by ` No Smoking` adverts. In the film the bus is seen operating fictitious route 72 and also travelling along Hyndland Street in the West End, which doesn't have a real bus route on it. Apart from filming in the city, the bus is also seen in the hills surrounding Loch Lomond.

Late January 1978 saw the almost new LA 1220 deroofed by the aqueduct that crosses the A81 just south of Ballat Crossroads in West Stirlingshire. The aqueduct carries water from Loch Katrine to Milngavie Waterworks for purification prior to being pumped into Glasgow's drinking water system. The bus had been on a private hire for an angling club and was heading for the Rob Roy Hotel when it encountered the 13 feet 6 inch high aqueduct. Seven passengers were injured, one seriously, in the accident which was caused by the driver straying off route. LA 1220 was converted to open top and gained a unique livery of all over yellow with a green skirt and a narrow white band above the lower deck windows. As new buses at the time qualified for 50% bus grant and LA 1220 had accumulated insufficient mileage, the bus appeared on the 77 Centre Circle service in June 1978. LA 1220 subsequently became a regular performer on this underused route. The bus even made it into the Glasgow Herald newspaper the following month under the headline` Shopping with the lid off`.

LA 1220 would later venture out on cross city routes and I can recall on more than one occasion seeing the bus at the Gairbraid Avenue end of service 26 from Toryglen. Together with LA 957 the bus was scrapped in November 1988 and was stripped of most reusable parts before onward sale to a dealer.

LA 1221 was sold by First Glasgow to the Health Board for use in the Vale of Leven area. Retaining SBL livery, the bus was parked at the back of the Polaroid factory on the Strathleven Industrial Estate. The author was surprised to discover the bus at this location in the summer of 1999. It should be remembered that apart from the Atlanteans sold to Michael Roulston, it was assumed that most of the final SBL Atlantean fleet had been sold for scrap. At the time I kept my knowledge of this bus quiet in case its discovery led to the bus being scrapped. With hindsight however, I would say that anyone finding a bus they feel should be saved ought to contact their local bus museum. Even if the bus is beyond saving, it may yield a valuable source of spare parts.

LA 1221 was initially bought for preservation by the Glasgow Bus Museum and initially it appeared that several people were interested in the bus. Over time the bus was cannibalised and by July 2003 the bus was parked at the rear of the closed Possilpark Garage awaiting collection for scrap by Dunsmore of Larkhall– a great shame as this was a saveable bus that through unfortunate circumstances was allowed to fall into it's final state. Indeed its interior could even have been used to restore LA 1204 to its original condition. A small consolation is that some parts from this bus were salvaged prior to scrapping to aid the restoration of LA 1443. LA 1230 had its engine shrouds partially cut away at the bottom, just above the engine compartment. Anyone familiar with a GGPTE Atlantean will know that this is a small fibre glass unit that sits on top of the engine cover. Quite why this unit was removed on some units and not others is not known but a number of Atlanteans were treated in this manner before the practice stopped, the altered Atlanteans subsequently being returned to their original condition.

LA 1238 was another Atlantean to be deroofed with Rigby Street in the east of the city the apparent scene of the accident.

LA 1251– 1310

LA 1251– 1310 FSU 68– 127T Leyland Atlantean AN68A/1R Alexander H45/33F
60 buses delivered between January and May 1979.

By August 1978 it was expected that deliveries of LA 1251– 1360, note 1360, would be at a rate of 3 buses per week. GGPTE was also expecting five Leyland Titans and five MCW Metrobuses, with deliveries of both of these chassis due to start in December 1978. It was anticipated that by operating these buses in service, the PTE would discover whether either would be suitable as a next generation replacement for the ageing Atlantean chassis.

LA 1251– 1310 differed from previous batches in several respects. The higher driving position and the larger offside driver's window being the most obvious. This latter alteration meaning the top of the cab window is in line with the top of the windscreen. On earlier deliveries, the top of the cab window was in line with the top of the offside saloon windows. An even more subtle change was the raising of the bottom edge of the windscreen to bring it into line with the lower deck windows. LA 1275– 80 were fitted from new with Firestone HELP energy absorbing pneumatic front bumpers that meant these buses were not fitted with front fog lights. Besides having the appearance of dodgem cars, LA 1275– 80 also had their front numberplates and fleetnumber plates relocated to non standard locations on the front panel. At the end of 1978 it became known that a new Trans-Clyde fleetname had been designed by Ogilvie, Benson and Mather(Scotland) Ltd. No public displays were noted of the new symbol until LA 1281 gained a white,

rather than black, Trans-Clyde fleetname for publicity reasons in August 1979.

LA 1285 took part in the commemorative service to mark the end of Glasgow Atlantean operation in June 1998. New to Ibrox Garage in May 1979, LA 1285 would be the final panoramic bodied Atlantean to operate in service with First Glasgow when it was withdrawn. The bus subsequently passed into preservation and although it was planned to restore the bus, it was sadly allowed to deteriorate and in the spring of 2004 it was sold to Dunsmore of Larkhall for scrap. As with LA 1221, some of the bus has been bought back to aid in the restoration of another preserved Atlantean. In this case LA 1324.

LA 1295 was the subject of various experiments prior to entering service. The bus was painted allover orange with a white band above the lower deck windows and finished with a Trans-Clyde fleetname. The shade of orange was similar to the shade used on the inter station Seddons and was a lighter shade of orange than the Strathclyde Red shade that later became fleet livery. The whole effect was similar to the livery being applied by City of Cardiff Transport at that time. Internally the bus was finished with a Tyne and Wear standard interior including moquette seating. When the bus finally entered service in October 1979 it was in standard GGPTE livery with GG fleetnames and a standard Glasgow interior.

LA 1272 heads south down Glassford Street in April 1995. Glasgow's Atlanteans running without foglights became a common sight in SBL days. An earlier style, LA 751– 1100, of window has been fitted to the second lower deck saloon window at some point as well. (B. Ridgway)

LA 1311–1350

LA 1311– 1350 LSU 368– 407V Leyland Atlantean AN68A/1R Alexander H45/33F
40 buses delivered between October 1979 and January 1980.

This batch is perhaps best known for two things, one being these buses were the last panoramic bodied Atlanteans bought new by the PTE and the other being the change to the destination display that saw the destination and service number being brought together in one display, although swapping positions from the previous deliveries. Note that the edge of the destination display was shaped rather than just being a rectangular hole cut in a sheet of aluminium.

Very much an intriguing batch that can be seen as either encompassing the last predominately Glasgow features in the Atlanteans or as being a trial run for the final 99 Atlanteans bought new, LA 1351– 1449. The former can be seen in the panoramic windows, LA 1350 was the 601st and final new panoramic body for the fleet with the use of green laminate on the interior panels and dark green vinyl seating. New features other than the destination display were the relocation of the heater intakes from either side of the rear numberplate to the space underneath the stairwell just behind the driver's cab. This naturally led to a simpler finish around the rear numberplate. The heater vents manifested themselves on the exterior immediately behind the driver's cab window. The fold down front, trialled earlier on LA 1140/51– 75 returned with LA 1311. Despite the new front panel affording easier access to the electrics, several buses were to receive older style front panels to the design used up until LA 1310, for example LA 1316/9/24/36, with LA 1319 being of note for receiving the alteration whilst still in PTE 3 livery. A less obvious change was to the driver's cab window with a three piece vertically sliding window replacing the previous smaller design. Illuminated OMO signs were introduced on Atlanteans with these buses.

Although found on Scottish Bus Group buses operating in the city, Glasgow had always tried a different approach when it came to informing the public that a bus was one man operated.

Sadly it appears that only LA 1324, of these buses, is still serviceable. LA 1321, which was the first bus to carry the new Strathclyde's Buses fleetname in July 1986, only just survives in a Lanarkshire scrapyard. As it has been shunted up the rear and had an engine placed on its roof, this is one bus, however, that is beyond saving, the only consolation being that it has donated parts to some of the preserved former Glasgow Atlanteans.

LA 1324 however is under restoration at Bus World in Renfrewshire after being bought by the author in late May 2004. After withdrawal by First Glasgow the bus saw a few months use with its GCT subsidiary prior to withdrawal from the fleet. After being stored at the former KCB garage in Old Kilpatrick, LA 1324 was amongst eight Atlanteans transferred to First Brewers/ First United Welsh. LA 1324 went to the later company and was the only one of the eight to get First United Welsh livery. In 1999 the bus was transferred within First Group to Western National. After a short period with this company the bus passed to Chepstow Classic Coaches from whom the author purchased the bus. This company has a storage facility at Winkleigh in Devon , just west of Exeter, from where LA 1324 made it's 478 mile trouble free trip back to Glasgow on the 7/8th June 2004. This bus and LA 1330 were rebuilt with short bay windows in the lower deck in 1981 when the PTE was trying to solve problem of body defects in its fleet of panoramic Atlanteans.

LA 1325, left, turns into Glassford Street from Ingram Street in June 1995 whilst on a post deregulation service to East Kilbride. The relocated heater grilles are not visible, but the restyled front dash and destination display stand out. (Brian. Ridgway)

LA 1351–1449

LA 1351– 1360 RDS 565– 574W Leyland Atlantean AN68A/1R Alexander H45/33F
LA 1361– 1385 RDS 540– 564W Leyland Atlantean AN68A/1R Alexander H45/33F
LA 1386– 1429 RDS 575– 618W Leyland Atlantean AN68A/1R Alexander H45/33F
LA 1430– 1439 SUS 598– 607W Leyland Atlantean AN68A/1R Alexander H45/33F
LA 1440/3/9 UGB 193/6/202W Leyland Atlantean AN68A/1R Alexander H45/33F
LA 1441/2/4– 8 CUS 296– 302X Leyland Atlantean AN68A/1R Alexander H45/33F

99 buses delivered between August 1980 and September 1981.

Prior to the delivery of this batch it was believed that 100 chassis were on order from Leyland. Whilst this was correct, it was erroneous to believe that all the buses were to be Atlanteans. When details of the buses involved became known, it was discovered that one of the chassis was a Leyland Olympian, LO 1. The last Atlanteans to be bought new for the fleet contrasted sharply with anything that had gone before. Short bay bodywork was back in vogue, problems with the panoramic bodies in the fleet having halted purchases of that variant of Alexander `AL` body. A two piece glider door replaced the previous four leaf door and the entrance platform now had a step. Internally the buses had moquette seating with brown laminate seatbacks. Laminate was used extensively throughout these buses in a cream and brown pattern that could be found on both decks. The destination display was enlarged to a similar style to that used on Tyne and Wear PTE Alexander bodied Atlanteans. Once again an intricate style was used around the outside edge of the destination display. When new, these buses had a top line display for destinations and a bottom line display for intermediate points with the service numbers remaining in situ on the offside. No buses ever ran in this format and although the top screen was used on its own for destinations, drivers found it difficult to set the screens properly and the top screen was blanked off. For a while the lower screen was used for destinations, but this also proved unsatisfactory. In the middle of 1982 moves were made to rebuild the displays in a single line destination alongside the service number, although LA 1393/ 1409/21 were to remain unaltered. As with the previous batch `Please pay driver` illuminated signs were displayed on the front panel when new, however as the route network was now 100% omo, the signs were superfluous and were later removed.

Mechanically, automatic gearboxes were ordered for these 99 buses instead of the PTE standard semi automatic gearbox. Air operated throttles were fitted instead of the mechanical linkage throttles used up until LA 1350. The combination of these two components adversely affected the ride quality on some of the buses with jerky gearchanges

LA 1387 with its upper destination screen in use and a front omo sign, sits between turns in Saint Enoch Square bus station. Note the `GG Trans– Clyde` fleetname on the between decks panel above the driver's cab. (David.G. Wilson)

and throttles a result. This last problem was caused by the drivers being unable to gauge when the accelerator had been pressed far enough down to allow the bus to move, leading to some drivers nicknaming these buses ` widow makers` for there ability to throw unsuspecting passengers around.

LA 1351– 60 should have arrived before August 1980 and registrations PHS 616– 25V were initially allocated to them. Delivery problems caused by a strike at Leyland, would delay LA 1440– 9. LA 1440/3/9 were initially licensed in May 1981 and were registered UGB 193/6/202W before being delicensed again. Had the whole batch been licensed simultaneously, LA 1441/2/4-8 would have received registrations UGB 194/5/7– 201W. The whole batch was noted at Leyland's service centre in Glasgow during June 1981, but it would be September 1981 before any of the buses actually entered service, by which time LA 1441/2/4- 8 had been re-registered CUS 296/7/9– 302X . However the original registrations were applied to some of the re-registered buses, with LA 1442 being delivered to Larkfield Garage carrying registration UGB195W. This suggests that the complete batch left Alexanders in Falkirk carrying UGB/W plates before being re-registered. This was to prove an academic exercise as the last Atlantean in service didn't come from these 10 buses.

The morning of the 2nd October 1985 saw LA 1401/31 involved in a head on crash in Old Mearns Road, Clarkston, that led to both buses being withdrawn. The two buses had been carrying schoolchildren to Mearns Castle High School that morning. At the time of the collision, one bus was returning empty to the Garage when it hit the other bus with twenty schoolchildren on board. Fifteen of the pupils were taken to hospital along with both drivers. The driver of the bus with the pupils on board had to be cut free by fireman, who took around twenty minutes to get him out. One resident who heard the collision said, `I heard a terrible bang and went to the front of the house`. The fact that both buses were subsequently written off suggests that this crash could have been a lot worse. Despite having the same type of seats as the rest of the batch, LA 1401/2 wore Coach Tour livery and were used on tours and hires from Larkfield Garage. After LA 1401 was written off, LA 1419 was transferred to Larkfield as its replacement and was repainted into coach livery by January 1986.

The last Atlantean to operate in passenger service in Glasgow was LA 1408 in November 1998. By the end it was supposed to be covering for buses that were off the road to be repainted into First Glasgow red, but nobody seems to have informed the staff at Knightswood Garage. Feedback from drivers who have driven this bus is interesting, some remember here as a jerky bus and others say it is a bit of a flyer. Regardless of this the bus didn't spend it's last few weeks in service idling away at the back of the garage or being used on crew transfers. LA 1408 was seen by the author moving up Crow Road towards Blairdardie on the 16 and by another enthusiast who observed it on a nocturnal hire in University Avenue just before its curtain call. This bus is currently in preservation and at the moment it is being kept in its final livery of SBL orange.

1983 saw the arrival of accessible public transport for the disabled in Glasgow using conventional buses. The concept was the brainchild of the then PTE`s director general, Alan Westwell. A couple of MCW Metroliners and some minibuses were adapted for wheelchair users as well as a quartet of Atlanteans. The first to appear, LA 1437, arrived in September 1983 with modifications that allowed

An attractively presented lady, well LA 1368 at any rate, stands at the kerbside in Cadogan Street whilst waiting on her next fare to arrive. Note that the lower destination display is now in use. This bus was delivered in PTE 1 livery and repainted into PTE 2 after delivery at the Bus Works. Compare this bus with the photo of LA 1427, which was finished in PTE 2 livery at the Alexander factory in Falkirk, on page 74. (David.G. Wilson)

it to carry wheelchairs on the `Chauffeur Care` network of services. To facilitate their new role the buses underwent major modifications, a feat that was further complicated by having to appease the Department of Transport with regard to the safety of using standard Atlanteans to carry several wheelchairs simultaneously. Wheelchair access to the lower saloon was via a ramp and outward opening doors that were inserted on the nearside where the second bay window in the lower saloon had been. As the batteries in this batch are positioned under the seats in the second and third rows on the nearside of the lower saloon, a cradle was built for the batteries underneath the floor so that wheelchairs could easily be manoeuvred within the bus. The modified lower deck could carry three wheelchairs and fifteen passengers who use seats at the rear of the lower saloon. These seats, however, had their moquette covers replaced by black vinyl during the conversion process. The service was aimed at the disabled and the bus carried a two man crew, one of whom helped wheelchair passengers on and off the bus. This obviously affected running times, which by necessity were longer than the parallel services alongside which these routes operated.

Initially, LA 1437 operated on service 61A, Argyle Street– Summerston, but soon services 62A, Argyle Street– Faifley, and 62B, Hope Street– Baillieston were added. By February 1984 LA 1436/40/2 had also been converted to the same standard as LA 1437 and all four buses could be found at work on both conventional and disabled services. At the time the PTE claimed they were the first operator to use conventional double deckers for this purpose. In February 1988 MCW Metroriders, M 72– 81 arrived in the fleet and these buses were built to accommodate wheelchairs via a wheelchair lift at the rear of the bus. This negated the need for LA 1436/7/40/2 and these were subsequently rebuilt in single door form. Although the buses regained a full complement of seats on the lower deck, all were of the black vinyl variety as opposed to the moquette they had when new.

LA 1440 which had been new to Parkhead Garage in October 1981 was deroofed by the railway bridge in Cook Street in the summer of 1985 and following repairs, the bus returned to service in October that year. In February 1997 this bus became one of only six former SPTE Atlanteans to carry First Glasgow red livery, complete with white fleetnames. This bus also took part in the Glasgow Atlantean farewell service in June 1998 along with LA 1/1285/1448. LA 1440 had been secured for preservation and carried a 1950`s style GCT livery, even having its moquette seating reinstalled in the lower deck. Sadly the bus was the victim of an arson attack whilst stored outside at the former Possilpark Garage and although the damage was confined to the lower deck, the survival of several other Atlanteans from this batch must place a question mark over its future. This would be sad as LA 1440 has a similar but non standard destination display in relation to the rest of the batch. This may be as a result of its bridge strike in 1985, but at some point the display has been rebuilt with the aperture cut straight out of the aluminium without the fancy moulding that was standard when new.

Another Atlantean that is now in preservation is LA

1443, the author and fellow preservationist Mark Budd having acquired this bus in June 2003 after much searching for a suitable Atlantean, the latter having taken the bus on himself since. It was only whilst trying to acquire the parts for this bus for its restoration that the unique qualities of this batch became apparent. Whilst the moquette and seatbacks were still available, the laminate used on the various side panels could only be purchased by removing it from another Atlantean. Fortunately LA 1442 was destined for the scrapyard and armed with a couple of wall paper scrapers and at least 4 tins of paint stripper, Mark managed to prise a strip of laminate from the side of LA 1442. The front panel on LA 1443 is also different from the one it had when new. The closest match still available would seem to be on the declining numbers of ex Grampian Atlanteans within First Group. None of these items would matter if it were not for the fact that the bus is to carry the SPTE third stage livery that it carried when new. Throughout 2004 the author had contacted various First Group subsidiaries that operated former Grampian Atlanteans, regarding purchasing a front panel from a redundant AN 68. Unfortunately the buses had always moved on to scrapyards by the time knowledge of their withdrawal became apparent. In December 2004 the author wrote in hope to First Group who were able to find a redundant Atlantean, NRS 311W, at its Livingston Garage. The fitting of this front to LA 1443 will allow LA 1324 to gain the front from LA 1443.

The bus itself was the last of the ex SPTE Atlanteans to gain First Glasgow red in July 1997 and carried grey Greater Glasgow fleetnames and fleetnumbers. Its final tax disc with First Group was valid until the end of March 1998, so it was not surprising that the bus was withdrawn on expiry of the disc. In May 2002 the final of the Champions League football tournament was staged at Hampden Park in Glasgow and LA 1443 gained adverts for Amstel beer, a prime sponsor of the 2001– 2 tournament, and was positioned in George Square along with a locally preserved red London Routemaster for use as publicity units prior to the final.

On account of the author moving a Kelvin Routemaster too close to LA 1445 at the bus stops under the Hielanman`s Umbrella in the summer of 1990, the bus is included in this book. Despite putting a hard right hand lock on to pull around LA 1445, I caught the Routemaster`s nearside wing mirror on the rear offside of the Atlantean above the engine shroud and left a trail of black rubber a few inches long. Fortunately, due to the slow speed involved, no damage was done and nobody apart from myself noticed; indeed to the casual eye it probably looked like some black paint had sneaked under the masking tape onto the orange. Unfortunately for me, SBL seemed to be in no hurry to repaint the bus and for several years afterwards I was reminded of my brush with it.

Just prior to withdrawal LA 1446 was reregistered TOS 968X. The mark, CUS 300X , being sold for use on a private car. The bus initially managed to escape the scrapyard and was last heard of a few years ago working as a driver trainer for a company on Merseyside.

The final Atlantean to enter service with Strathclyde PTE was LA 1448 which started working from Langside Garage in October 1981. The bus which is now in preservation has retained its final SBL livery and First Greater Glasgow fleetnames. According to drivers who have driven this bus it is a bit of a slug. In recent years the bus has attended the `Western Scottish Leyland Leopard` farewell at Dumfries in May 2001 and the 2002 Scottish Vintage Bus Museum Open Day at Lathalmond.

Numerically, the last new Atlantean for SPTE was LA 1449. Attempts were made to secure this bus for preservation, but as with LA 664, the bus was dispatched to the breakers yard in error. First Glasgow had planned to eliminate Atlantean operation by the end of March 1998, but due to the number of vehicles requiring repainting into the new red livery this was postponed. The 2nd of May and then the 6th of June were the dates proposed for a celebration of the type. The problem was that LA 1449 was sold into preservation prior to the 2nd of May and First Glasgow wanted to retain the bus until it had participated in the farewell celebrations. With the ceremony being postponed again until June, the bus was dispatched to Wigley, dealer of Carlton, who broke the bus up before its mistaken dispatch had been discovered.

LA 1449 may have been the highest numbered new Atlantean in the fleet, but it wasn't the last new Atla ntean into service. LA 1449 heads east along Argyle Street with an Alexander bodied Volvo Citybus following behind on a Sunday in May 1994. Note that the second window on the offside lower deck of LA 1449 has lost its vent for plain glass. (B. Ridgway)

LA 1450– 1456

LA 1450– 1454 OTO 554/61/6/7/81M Leyland Atlantean AN68/1R East Lancs H45/33F
LA 1455/6 JAL 877/9N Leyland Atlantean AN68/1R East Lancs H45/34F

In June 1992 these seven buses, notable for their unusual East Lancs bodywork, became the first secondhand Atlanteans to be purchased by SBL or any of its predecessors. Technically the ex Busways Atlanteans were on the road first, but they spent their first few months in Glasgow on loan to SBL. LA 1450– 6 had been new to Nottingham as 554/61/6/7/81/607/9 and had arrived in Glasgow as dual door buses, LA 1450– 4 had been H47/30D and LA 1455/6 had been H47/31D with Nottingham. Prior to entering service the buses underwent conversion to single door and were repainted into standard fleet livery. The conversion work being undertaken at both Larkfield Garage and bodybuilder, Bennett of Springburn. In the lower saloon, a three seat bench was put in the space at the former centre door platform. Upstairs between the stairwell and the windscreen there had been two forward facing double seats as well as an inward facing double seat. The inward facing seat was removed and the double seat nearest the windscreen was rotated to face into the upper saloon.

The buses were not well received by the crews with poorly laid out cabs and reflective problems with the windscreen amongst the complaints. These problems were small fry when compared with the fault the drivers` union picked upon. Prior to arriving in Glasgow the buses had been retro-fitted with Autosteer power steering. This didn't meet with the union's approval as it was felt that the steering was inadequate. When the buses were going round sharp corners the buses were not as responsive as they should have been and gave drivers the impression that the bus was out of control. This led to the buses being blacked by the union until SBL had an acceptable power steering system fitted.

LA 1453/4 entered service from Parkhead Garage in August 1992 and by October they had been joined by LA 1450– 2 as regular performers on service 61, Summerston – Tollcross. LA 1455/6 were put to work the same month from Larkfield Garage on various routes. All seven buses were transferred to GCT on its formation in August 1993 as GLA 4– 10. Some of the buses operated for a while during July 1993 in GCT livery with Strathclyde's Buses fleetnames on their fronts; whilst with GCT LA 1452/4/5 would be rebuilt with Alexander AL style upper front domes, which necessitated the widening of the front window pillars.

The ex-Nottingham Atlanteans bought in the aftermath of the Larkfield fire were the first secondhand `LAs` for the fleet, they wouldn't be the last! LA 1453 is seen heading west in Argyle Street not long after entering service with Strathclyde Buses. (A. Douglas)

LA 1457– 1466

LA 1457/8 JVK 234/8P Leyland Atlantean AN68A/1R Alexander H45/31F
LA 1459– 66 MVK 502/6/8/12/6/28/52/67R Leyland Atlantean AN68A/2R Alexander H48/33F

Initially, these buses operated for two months, from June till August 1992, on loan to Strathclyde Buses from Busways, as C 930– 9, before being purchased. The buses were allocated to Larkfield Garage and entered service on the 2/3 June 1992 on services 21, Kessington– Pollok, and 45 ,Auchinairn– Kennishead. Unlike other hired in buses, these vehicles had their lower deck panels and windows repainted into SBL livery as well as their fronts and rears. So short of buses was SBL that some of these buses were put to work in Glasgow with Newcastle adverts for a short time. Once the buses had been purchased in August they received fleetnumbers LA 1457– 66 as well as full SBL livery. By the time of their purchase it was also becoming clear that their actual seating layouts did not match their listed configurations, given above. LA 1459– 61/6 were actually H48/34F, LA 1462 was H48/30F, LA 1463 was H48/31F, leaving only LA 1457/8/65 to be laid out as listed above. This confusion probably has its origins in LA 1459– 66 having been rebuilt from dual door to single door layout on Tyneside, the former centre door platform being replaced by seating.

Despite having similar panoramic bodies to the Glasgow examples, any rivet counter, (nasty word), will be able to tell you the Busways Atlanteans were radically different to anything Glasgow had ever bought. Most obvious was the lack of engine shrouds on the Busways vehicles and some also retained their protruding headlamps, similar to the style seen on resident LA 1083 when new. LA 1459– 66 had all been dual door when new and had their stairwell located over the front nearside axle.

As with LA 1351– 1449 all the ex Busways stock had moquette seating in a style that incorporated the Tyne and Wear PTE symbol. Laminate was used extensively in these buses with the side panels in the lower saloon having the style of laminate that was later used by GGPTE in the LA 1351– 1449 batch, the seat backs and upper deck using a different style of laminate. The Tyne and Wear PTE symbol was also used in the ceiling panels on both decks as were Edinburgh style lights. The destination display had been used in two track mode in Newcastle, but as with LA 1351– 1449 only the lower track was used in Glasgow. A typical Glasgow feature was a side number box on the nearside. Despite

their age the overall condition of the buses was good, but to the consternation of SBL drivers, their previous owner had the doors wired so that they couldn't be opened when the bus was in gear. This wasn't the only problem affecting time keeping, Busways had also set the buses so that first, or crawler, gear had to be selected to pull away. SBL subsequently changed the gearboxes so that second gear could be selected for pulling away, incidentally these buses had a gas cooker type switch for selecting the gear. LA 1457/8 had four leaf doors and were standard length, 31 ft, Atlanteans, as were LA 1467/8, the rest of the Busways AN 68s had two leaf doors. LA 1459– 66 were the first 33 feet Atlanteans to operate in the fleet, although technically they were 32 feet 10 inches long and had a wheelbase of 18 feet 6 inches. The extra length was identified in the chassis code as the number `2`. In contrast a Glasgow Atlantean was 30 feet 10 inches long with a wheelbase of 16 feet 3 inches. For those who wouldn't know a rivet from a nail, the longer buses were easily identifiable by having five windows upstairs and three windows downstairs on their offsides, which was one window more on each deck than a resident example. It may not be obvious, but the author owns an anorak.

As with the ex Nottingham buses, all the Busways Atlanteans were transferred to GCT on its formation in August 1993 with LA 1457– 66 becoming GLA 11– 20.

The above image finds soon to be LA 1466 loading in Renfield Street. The bus not only retains some of its former Busways livery, but a between decks advert for a Newcastle business is evident. (Billy Nicol)

LA 1467–1476

LA 1467/8 JVK 235/6P Leyland Atlantean AN68A/1R Alexander H45/31F
LA 1469– 71 MVK 520/7/50R Leyland Atlantean AN68A/2R Alexander H48/33F
LA 1472– 76 VCU 305/7/8/11/3T Leyland Atlantean AN68A/2R Alexander H49/37F

In October 1992 Strathclyde Buses returned to Busways and purchased another ten Atlanteans to allow the return of some of the buses borrowed after the Larkfield Fire. LA 1467– 76 all entered service in full SBL livery and it goes without saying that the P and R registration examples are identical to those described in the previous chapter. LA 1472– 6 however added yet another variant to the fleet. Whilst 33 feet long, these buses had their staircase in the traditional offside position over the front axle. This change led to all three windows on the offside of the lower saloon being of different lengths. LA 1474– 6 had H.E.L.P energy absorbing bumpers as fitted to resident LA 1275– 80. Unlike the Glasgow examples, LA 1474– 6 did not have the high driving position for the steering wheel or the larger offside cab window. Initial allocations for this batch being:-

Knightswood LA 1467– 9/72
Parkhead LA 1470
Possilpark LA 1471/3– 6
When the buses joined the GCT fleet in August 1993 they became GLA 21– 30.

LA 1477–1483

LA 1477/8 JVK 240/3P Leyland Atlantean AN68A/1R Alexander H45/31F
LA 1479 MVK 503R Leyland Atlantean AN68A/2R Alexander H48/34F
LA 1480 MVK 529R Leyland Atlantean AN68A/2R Alexander H48/33F
LA 1481 SCN 272S Leyland Atlantean AN68A/2R Alexander H49/31F
LA 1482/3 UVK 293/6T Leyland Atlantean AN68A/2R Alexander H49/31F

The final seven former Busways Atlanteans arrived from Tyneside in December 1992 and as with the previous batch were put to work after they had received full fleet livery. In total 27 Atlanteans, all with panoramic bodies, were purchased from Busways. This brought the number of panoramic bodied Atlanteans bought for the fleet to 628. LA 1477– 80 were as described for previous vehicles from the same batches. LA 1481– 3 had their staircases in the traditional offside position and as with the previous `T` registered examples, LA 1482/3 had the lower driving position for the steering wheel. Initial allocations being :-

Knightswood LA 1477/8/82
Parkhead LA 1479– 81/3
On transfer to GCT at it's formation the buses became GLA 31– 7.

It wasn't just Greater Glasgow that ordered Atlanteans fitted with HELP bumpers as this former Busways example illustrates. GLA 29 is seen in Glasgow Road in Paisley whilst working for GCT. Unlike the Glasgow examples with `T` registration plates, these buses retained the steering wheel in the lower driving position. (A.J. Douglas)

LA 538– 551, Deja Vu

LA 538 VET 606S Leyland Atlantean AN68A/1R Roe H45/29D
LA 539 CWG 720V Leyland Atlantean AN68A/1R Alexander H45/29D
LA 540/1 CWG 771/2V Leyland Atlantean AN68A/1R Roe H45/29D
LA 542/3 JKW 319/29W Leyland Atlantean AN68B/1R Marshall H45/29D
LA 544– 51 WAG 370/81/78/3/4/9/6/7 X Leyland Atlantean AN68C/1R Roe H43/31F

These fourteen buses were the first Atlanteans to be purchased after the privatisation of Strathclyde Buses. The buses had been bought in October 1994 when it looked as though Stagecoach was going to start cross city operations in Glasgow. Indeed Stagecoach even went so far as to register the operations before a deal was struck between Strathclyde Buses and Stagecoach. Apart from Stagecoach acquiring a 20% holding of the privatised SBL, they also sold eighteen brand new Alexander 'PS' bodied Volvo B10Ms to SBL. It is believed that LA 538– 51 had originally been purchased for use on competitive services against Stagecoach in either Fife or Perth. With this need negated, the buses stayed out of sight for several months and LA 538/49 were even rumoured to be heading for GCT as GLA 50/1; indeed LA 549 gained GCT livery but was never operated by that subsidiary.

In the spring of 1995 all fourteen buses were allocated to the Kelvin Central subsidiary where besides gaining the standard KCB livery, they were given fleetnumbers 1924–37. When the fleetnumber system was revised so that all SBL subsidiaries were using the same codes, these buses mysteriously became LA 538– 51 instead of the expected LA 1484– 97.

LA 538– 43 had all originated with South Yorkshire PTE, although prior to their purchase by SBL, LA 538 was with Cedar Coaches of Bedford, LA 539 was with Swift of Blaxton and LA 540– 3 were with SYPTE's successor Mainline. Perhaps reflecting the age and expected life of LA 538– 41, the dual door buses were not rebuilt to single door, instead they had their centre doors blocked off and replaced by a sign telling passengers 'This is not a door, no entrance', which no doubt confused many passengers.

LA 544– 51 had all come from Hull where following the purchased of that city's fleet by Stagecoach, the Atlanteans had been sold off. Although not as attractive as the Alexander body, these were fine buses and it is pleasing to record that LA 550 was bought by a preservationist from Hull during 2003 after operating with Aberdeenshire operator, Burns of Tarves. LA 547/9 were loaned within First Group to Midland Bluebird in early 1998, with LA 549 being sold to that concern in April 1998 and becoming 759. In May 2002 the bus was transferred within First Group to First Northampton, but only as a source of spares.

As these buses only operated for Kelvin their claim to be Glasgow Atlanteans appears to be spurious. It is true that none of the buses wore SBL livery or even First Glasgow red and none had their own unique fleetnumber. However after the closure of Kirkintilloch Garage some of the buses were allocated to the KCB unit at Possilpark Garage and following the closure of Old Kilpatrick Garage in 1996 some were sent to the KCB unit at Knightswood Garage.

Marshall bodied Atlantean 1928 leaves Buchannan Bus Station in April 1995. The similarities in bodywork style to Citybus AH 1 and Ailsas A117/8 are noticeable. (B. Ridgway)

LA 1450–1453, again!

LA 1450-2 HSO 282/6/90V Leyland Atlantean AN68A/1R Alexander H45/29D
LA 1453 LRS 291W Leyland Atlantean AN68A/1R Alexander H45/29D

LA 1450-3 – note the reissued fleetnumbers – initially arrived on loan from First Aberdeen in May 1997 and were put to work with the Kelvin unit based at Knightswood Garage on crew transport and contract services. The following month saw the buses purchased by First Glasgow and by October 97 they had received First Glasgow red as well as having their centre doors removed to become H45/31F.

This particular type of Alexander body, short bay windows, dual doors with peaked front and rear domes, had been seen in the fleet before when C 924– 8 had been on loan from GRT Holdings in 1992. LA 1450– 3, however, were the first Atlanteans with this style of bodywork to be owned by First Glasgow or any of its predecessors and they were also the last Atlanteans to be bought for the fleet. LA 1450– 3 were actually Atlanteans 1498– 1501 and ended a chain that had begun 39 years previously in December 1958 with LA 1.

Whilst reasons could be found to justify the purchase of the previous fourteen Atlanteans, none, or at least any reasons that withstood scrutiny, could be found to justify these four buses. LA 538– 51 were bought when a competitor had appeared on the horizon and even when this failed to materialise they found use by eliminating Ailsas and Fleetlines from the SBL group. A possible reason for LA 1450– 3 being justified is that there was a shortage of buses in the fleet. The reason there was a shortage of buses in the fleet was because someone had seen fit to withdraw, on mass, resident Atlanteans or transfer early ECW bodied Leyland Olympians to Eastern Counties. In August 1997 four Glasgow Atlanteans were transferred to First Group subsidiaries Brewers and South Wales. Eight LA s in total would be transferred to South Wales although some went to Wales only for cannibalisation of parts. One, LA, 1324, subsequently saw use with First Western National and two of the Atlanteans sent to Wales outlived their colleagues left in Glasgow by several years. Some observers might have sent the Grampian buses straight to Wales and thus eliminated one set of repaints from the equation.

Whilst only six Glasgow Atlanteans received First Glasgow red, all four of these buses were repainted into red. I remember seeing LA 1450 in Crow Road on service 16 and it certainly looked smart. It was assumed that after all the attention these buses had received there was a future for them in Glasgow, but by September 98 only LA 1452/3 were still operational and neither of these lasted as long as resident LA 1408. Stranger still, given the propensity of ex-Grampian Atlanteans that found work elsewhere in First Group, is that LA 1450-3 were scrapped rather than transferred within First Group.

LA 1450 passes through Anniesland Cross having gained First Glasgow red and a single door.
The bus has also picked up two different rear view mirrors at some point. (A.J. Douglas)

OMO : The conversion programme

One man operation, omo, was introduced to Glasgow in 1965 using Alexander bodied Leyland Panther LS 31 operating service 40 to Hillington. By August 1965 following several months of inactivity after a couple of accidents, it was operating service 21, Midland Street– Pollok. The next omo bus, LS 32, joined it on the 21 road in February 1966. The back up vehicle at this time was Leyland Royal Tiger Worldmaster LS 26. These omo buses wore reverse livery to distinguish them from the rest of the fleet.

In 1967 agreement was reached to operate omo double deckers, GCT believed this an important breakthrough in the conversion programme. As noted elsewhere in this book the first Atlantean converted for omo was LA 362. It was felt that omo would lead to a substantial reduction in the ratio of wages to costs. An omo driver got paid more than a crew driver because of the extra responsibilities single manning entailed, but less than a driver and conductor combined. The Glasgow Herald of 26th June 1968 reported that drivers of LA 362 received 25% extra pay and an extra 20% for driving the omo Panthers. This increase in pay, GCT thought, would lead to a higher standard of applicant for drivers positions. Ultimately this would lead to a reduction in the problems of maintaining the network which at this point in time was struggling because of staff shortages. GCT and the unions had an agreement, but all was not well. Only two buses could operate without a conductor at any given time. In a fleet of around 1300 buses, this hardly represented progress. Negotiations continued with the aim of a more rapid and widespread introduction of omo buses. Despite the obstacles GCT felt that a workable omo system could be introduced. It admitted that the problems appeared overwhelming but the potential benefits such as an improvement in productivity could only be achieved by single manning. GCT also felt that a great deal of investigation, thought and radical alteration might be required to the route and fare systems if the conductor was to be permanately removed from the bus. There were also physical problems and with this in mind GCT was in touch with the Ministry of Transport regarding their regulations. Talks took place regarding subjects like reversing lights, audible warnings and other amendments required to comply with omo. Reversing of buses troubled GCT and it decided that routes that didn't involve reversing or could be rerouted to avoid this manoeuvre at termini would be converted to omo first.

Mr Fitzpayne reported to the transport committee on the 21st August 1968 that, ` double deck omo operation is possible, but successful operation can only be achieved with dual door buses.` Although the first dual door Atlantean, LA 422, had by then been delivered, it did not enter service until November that year. GCT was however operating dual door Panthers and single door Atlanteans on omo route 21 and it would seem likely that the experience gained from this service was giving valuable information on the need for an extra door in the lower saloon. 1969 saw GCT standardise on the dual door Atlantean and in 1970 it reported that, ` the introduction of dual door buses reduces the time spent at bus stops where there is boarding and alighting conflict.` It is therefore ironic that GGPTE set about ripping the second door out of these buses from 1974 onwards and went back to single door buses for the remainder of Atlantean deliveries. Even more ironic is that PTE supremo Ronald Cox had been the man who had introduced the dual door Atlantean to Edinburgh.

However this episode is viewed, mistakes were made. Maybe dual doors were the way to go and the PTE got it wrong or maybe the PTE got it right and GCT got it wrong. Regardless of who got it right, this wouldn't be the only time that valuable cash was wasted on omo projects that made negligible or no improvement to the drivers on the street.

The green light for unlimited double deck omo operation was finally given by the union and on the 2nd February 1969 services 21 and 39 were converted to 100% omo operation. Services 17 and 25 being changed to 100% double deck omo operation on 23rd February 1969. By May that year 46 buses were operating seven omo services and plans were provisionally agreed to have 100 buses operating twelve omo routes by December 1969. Indeed at this point in time, it was GCT`s aim to have all services that didn't operate through the city centre converted to omo. A common complaint amongst the public was that the Corporation's buses weren't as well illuminated as the trams had been and with this in mind GCT stated that omo buses were to get fluorescent lighting. The conversion of Atlanteans for OMO was most likely to occur when the buses were in for overhaul and by the end of May 1969 123 periscopes had been manufactured at the Bus Works for Atlanteans. In an example of patting its own back, GCT reported that these periscopes were better than anything else that could be bought and crucially they were popular with drivers. The Bus Works was also responsible for the manufacture of cab alteration parts for omo buses like cash trays and ticket machine holders. To enlighten the public that there was no conductor on the approaching Atlantean, a large red dot was painted on the front dome of the bus. The only drawback with this approach was that by necessity omo Atlanteans were sometimes allocated to crew routes and there was no means available to cover the dot. This was the first, but it wouldn't be the last initiative for omo buses that would comeback and haunt management.

The unions and the Ministry of Transport weren't the

only obstacles to be overcome, there were logistical issues as well. Cross city omo buses were a concern for GCT. Whilst suburban buses rarely had to deal with the heavy loads of the city routes, routes that terminated in the city centre rarely had equal numbers of passengers trying to alight and board simultaneously, this was not the case with cross city routes. Only at their suburban termini could these routes be guaranteed no serious passenger conflict on the platform. With no conductor to collect fares on route, the potential for jams was greatest on these routes and it was obvious that the conversion of cross city routes to omo was going to be a mammoth task. On May 16th 1970 service 60, Maryhill– Shettleston, became the first proper cross city route to be converted to omo. By the end of the month 183 buses had been converted to omo with nine of the city's eleven garages were involved with omo routes. A significant event occurred on June 6th 1971 when Langside Garage became the first garage to be a conductor free zone.

Fare collection was a time consuming affair that badly needed overhauling, drivers being hindered at bus stops by Ultimate barrel ticket machines and a cash tray. In an attempt to speed up boarding LA 466– 81 were fitted with Bell Autoslot passenger operated ticket machines in February 1970 for use on service 28, on which buses were travelling around four miles from the City Centre to Milton on the northern edge of Glasgow. Whilst this sounds like an improvement, the new equipment was not as revolutionary as the management hoped it would be. The initial optimism within GCT soon evaporated and by 1973 it was felt that the Autoslot system was underperforming. In the end it wasn't much of a surprise that by July 1973 the Autoslots were gone and the Ultimate barrel machines would last another six years. It is unfortunate that the shortcomings of the Autoslot system weren't addressed as the use of cash trays left drivers vulnerable to the theft of their takings for several years to come.

By April 1974 only a few crew routes that were suitable for conversion to omo remained to be addressed. The `turning circle` and `loops` were to become important tools in converting less suitable routes. A turning circle was built at Acre Road and with the truncating of service 1 from Killermont to Acre Road during 1976, a problematic reversing manoeuvre at the former terminus was removed from the route. Indeed the transport committee had discussed moving this terminus off Maryhill Road to nearby Corporation land in the summer of 1959. With the awkward routes now being addressed it was only a matter of time before 100% omo operation of the PTE`s buses arrived. In later years buses were sent on loops of left or right hand turns at termini, Darnley, Kessington and Summerston being a few examples.

The conversion programme continued under GGPTE ownership and in the PTE`s first year in charge omo rose to 59% of all routes with a further five crew routes converted. Indeed more routes would have been changed had the delivery of new vehicles not been delayed by circumstances out with the PTE`s control. On the 15th September 1974 the first truly successful omo aid was introduced and apart from reducing the need for drivers to issue tickets and handle cash, there were noticeable improvements in

timekeeping. The four weekly Transcard offered unlimited travel on Executive buses and the underground with the exemption of night buses. At £6 for adults and £3 for children the tickets proved popular with the public with sales rising rapidly from 7 000 tickets per month in 1974 to nearly 37 000 tickets by May 1976. The 23rd of October 1977 saw the weekly Transcard go on sale and in connection with this LA 995 gained an all over advert for Transcard tickets.

During 1977/8 management and staff were in talks regarding a new method of fare collection. Crews at Knightswood were demanding greater protection and had mentioned `no change` systems to management. The PTE would have rather found a better alternative knowing that passengers would object to such a system. The favoured system amongst the crews at Knightswood was the Autofare system, but the PTE had several systems inspected. It was anticipated that the new equipment would be ordered during 1978 for delivery around the end of the year. To this end two new buses had Almex, LA 1215, and Autofare, LA 1217, equipment temporarily fitted to demonstrate the no change system, but the two buses reverted to the Ultimate ticket system prior to entering service. In the end the Almex `E` ticket system was chosen to replace the Ultimate machines and in preparation for the new system's introduction LA 637 was used as an experimental Almex fare collection bus in trials commencing December 1978. A strike at the Bus Works would delay the fitting of the new machines to any buses, but prior to the launch of the new system LA 1062 was painted as an all over advert for `Fast Fare` in May 1979 and demonstrated how the new system worked. As part of the publicity campaign aimed at the public, a cartoon character `Freddie Fast Fare` was devised to catch the eye of the public.

The 17th June 1979 saw the Fast Fare system introduced on routes 41/71/91 from Gartcraig Garage in the north east of the city in a phased conversion planned to last 18 months. With the red coin vault placed on the front platform next to the driver and Almex ticket machine, Fast Fare was the final nail in the coffin for crew operation on the city's buses. 58 buses at Gartcraig and 31 buses at Knightswood had been fitted for Fast Fare by the middle of September and the end of crew operation occurred on the 12th of December 1979 when route 59 was converted to omo Ultimate operation. However not everything was going to plan, Service 44 which had been converted to Fast Fare at the end of 1979 was converted back to crew operation during January 1980 due to a shortage of buses fitted with the new equipment. By the end of March 1980, 15 years after LS 31 and 13 years after LA 362, the fleet finally became 100% omo operation with Almex fareboxes now fitted to half of the fleet. The effects on the public of the change to Fast Fare were that instead of a multitude of tickets being issued for a journey, Fast Fare issued just one ticket. There was also the matter of having the exact fare for the buses. With no change given on the buses, the public were faced with several choices if they didn't tender the exact fare;- they could travel as far as available money would allow, they could pay slightly more than their fare required and forget the change or they could overpay for the fare and get a refund from the PTE. As this last option required the passenger travelling to PTE offices

In the later Corporation era and early days of the PTE, a large board below the driver's windscreen proclaimed that the bus was one man operated. LA 691, above, is seen in the city centre with the then still new `GG` logo. (David.G.Wilson)

As LA 1055, above, in Corkerhill Road demonstrates, the next aid for identifying one man operated buses was the placing of the `Please Pay Driver` board in the upper left part of the lower deck windscreen. This bus also has fog lamp rings, an unusual occurrence on a Glasgow Atlantean. (David.G. Wilson)

HELP bumper fitted LA 1278 sits in the City Centre. The notice in the windscreen tells passengers that service 41 and a number of other routes operating from Gartcraig Garage have been converted to the No Change `Fast Fare` system. Just visible below this notice is the cash vault. Note how the addition of the HELP bumper to LA 1275– 80 led to the towing eyes been raised to a non standard location. (David.G. Wilson)

LA 703 in Strathclyde Transport livery loads at Govan bus Station. The exact fare viynls below the windscreen have been replaced by a small white rectangular vinyl above the front nearside indicator with the same message. In the background one of the pre-production Mark One Ailsas can be seen. (David.G. Wilson)

in the city centre this wasn't a much used option. Thus the public settled into a habit of paying a few pence too much for their journey and the PTE saw below target weigh ins, caused by crews incorrectly giving passengers too much change, reduced.

The PTE also had to adjust to the new system. Infrastructure changes were implemented at garages as new maintenance and cash handling procedures were introduced. At the garages new cash handling centres were introduced which involved building alterations and the PTE had to develop a new bulk cash handling scheme. At no stage would the drivers come into contact with any cash, drivers were not to give passengers change for the vaults and they were not to release jammed vaults themselves. This development was actually a good thing as there was a noticeable drop in assaults on staff for cash after Fast Fare was introduced. In subsequent years the PTE noticed a drop in it's staff shortage and it is believed the use of vaults played a part in attracting and retaining staff.

In early 1983 the PTE ordered 33 Timtronic electronic ticket machines for evaluation purposes. Some were fitted to Ailsas at Larkfield Garage for use on service 12 and the rest were fitted to Atlanteans based at Knightswood Garage for use on service 20. Some of the Atlanteans involved being LA 1240/52/83/1449. Whilst the use of Timtronic machines didn't progress beyond the trial, another trial with Wayfarer ticket machines proved more successful, eventually. Wayfarer machines in their early days printed the tickets on a small white rectangle of plain paper, unlike the large tickets that are issued today. Whilst most of the machines used were similar to the Wayfarer ticket machines used today, some Atlanteans had an experimental ticket machines fitted to them. To the public the buses used were like every other bus in the fleet, except that the issued ticket didn't come out of the ticket machine but out of a small slot in the stair bulkhead behind the driver's cab. Having had the misfortune to board one such LA one day on the 57 to Ruchill, I can understand why this ticket system was rejected. Having put my money in the vault I then spent about a minute listening to increasingly desperate directions from the driver as I tried to locate the ticket. By the time I got my ticket I was wishing I hadn't stopped what quite clearly was a bus from hell, only to see the whole episode repeated at each subsequent stop. With the consequent effect to running times I would assume it didn't take much of a defect for drivers to attempt to sign this bus of the road. Not surprisingly when the Wayfarer machines became standard on SPTE buses the ticket was issued at the ticket machine.

August 1984 finds PTE 3 liveried LA 1246 in Hope Street at Central Station. Careful inspection of the windscreen to the left of the driver reveals an early Wayfarer ticket machine. (David.G. Wilson)

Poor Defect Rate

An unfortunate consequence of using buses in service is that sooner or later they are going to break down. It follows therefore that someone, a mechanic or engineer, will have to be employed to repair the defective buses. Whilst day to day checks and repairs could be done at any garage, the major repairs like overhauls and serious accident damage were sent to Larkfield Bus Works. As is well known the Glasgow Atlantean had more than its fair share of problems.

During the 12 months prior to May 1968, LA 15 became the first standard Atlantean, LA 1 wasn't standard, to undergo an overhaul and this is reflected in the fact that it took 1035 hours just to overhaul the body. Despite such a high figure, it was felt that as overhaul times varied greatly within groups of vehicles, it could not be taken as a guide for the future cost of overhauls. This figure was substantially above what would be considered normal for smaller double deck buses, but it must be remembered that prior to this time, Atlanteans had only received attention to damaged or defective parts of the vehicle. Never before had the mechanics gone to work on a complete standard Atlantean, so mistakes would be made and lessons learned for future overhauls. By May 1969 there had been 47 Atlanteans overhauled and in just over a year 300 hours had been saved in the time taken to overhaul these buses, although this was still 181 hours higher than smaller capacity vehicles. However, the problems weren't confined to overhauls of the body, similar excess hours were also being noted against electrical and mechanical overhauls.

By May 1970 120 Atlanteans had been overhauled and the average time of an overhaul was down to 685 hours, but even this remained in excess of the time needed to overhaul smaller vehicles. During the overhauls a serious defect in the design of the PDR Atlantean was manifesting itself with metal corrosion of the twin fuel tanks being found. The extent of the corrosion varied from bus to bus, but many tanks were found to be beyond repair. A solution was found and the fuel tanks were coated with fibre glass before being refitted to the chassis. It was anticipated that this remedial action would see the need for further attention to the tanks during the lifetime of the vehicle being negated.

Overheating of PDR Atlanteans was a notorious problem and Glasgow's had more then their share of the problem. An overheated engine is a major problem, as besides the vehicle having to stop, there is the knock on effect of this stoppage in the schedules and also, depending where the breakdown occurred, the potential for disruption of other road traffic. There is also the chance of an engine seizeure due to lack of water and the consequent extreme heat with a shortage of coolant. Design faults within the bus were at the root of the problem and such was the build up of heat under the bonnet that the bench seat across the rear of the lower saloon often would heat up. In extreme cases the lower deck ceiling and rear window surround had deposits of soot due to some of the buses allowing exhaust fumes to enter the rear lower saloon. Not all the problems were of Leyland's making however; traffic congestion in pre-motorway Glasgow wasn't helping either. In 1966 on difficult evenings it could take a bus 40 minutes to travel the mile between Charing Cross and Argyle Street via Sauchiehall Street and Renfield Street and during October 1967 it took 66 minutes for one bus to travel this distance. Whilst these incidences don't specifically relate to Atlanteans it would be difficult to imagine that Atlanteans were the only buses in the fleet not getting caught up in these traffic jams. GCT was worried about the congestion for the effects it was having on its fleet, stating that, ` slow running for long periods in congested conditions seriously impairs the mechanical efficiency of our vehicles.` Of course defects were not confined to the Atlanteans, but the LA was rapidly becoming the backbone of the fleet. GCT had to do something to improve the reliability of its Atlantean fleet by making changes, some more subtle than others, to its PDRs to stop them overheating. The most obvious to the naked eye was the emergence of large areas of mesh on the rear engine cover. LA 205 was one bus to be treated, including the cutting of two small holes at the base of the engine cover. Despite increasing the amount of air getting under the bonnet this didn't stop the overheating and yet more holes were cut in the bonnets, but to no avail. Less obvious was the enlarging of the radiator grille to allow for more cooling of the engine. Additionally the gearbox and angle drive casing were drilled to allow an improved flow of oil from the angle drive casing back to the gearbox.

With all that heat under the bonnet, fire was a possibility. Components under the bonnet that became soaked in oil were also subject to the regular excessive heat emanating from the engine. The engineers at GCT were troubled by this and in an effort to reduce this likelihood, the undersides of posts and the engine covers within the compartment were treated with Fire Resistant Polyester Instumescent, FRPI. The FRPI had a British Standard Grade Rating of 1 and such were its fire inhibiting qualities that when fibreglass treated with FRPI was exposed to a naked flame, it failed to ignite.

Ironically with all these worries about heat and fire, it should transpire that the early Atlanteans were suffering problems with airlocks in the heater pipe systems. Modifications were made to eliminate the air locks and this consequently improved the performance of both the heaters and the demisters. By the end of May 1971 485 of the 550 Atlanteans in service had been treated.

The difficulties of keeping the rear engine vehicles in

a satisfactory standard was a concern and GCT felt their reliability was below par, although as already noted, improvements and rectifications were being made in Glasgow. However not all the problems could be solved locally and for this Leyland is partly to blame. 57 Atlanteans were off the road in January 1970 because of a shortage of gearbox parts. In order to overcome future problems with availability of spare parts, GCT threatened to part cancel its order for 150 Atlanteans due to commence in June 1970 with LA 501. Spare parts were not the only concern; nationally the shortage of Atlantean chassis was causing problems and having an order with Leyland really wasn't worth the paper it was written on. That you would get your buses wasn't the problem, the problem was that Leyland could be a little economical with the truth where delivery dates were concerned. Besides Leyland, GCT was also in touch with other operators throughout Britain in a bid to gain more knowledge of the problems afflicting Atlanteans. An example of this is when Greater Manchester 7070, VNB 170L, a 1972 Park Royal bodied AN 68, visited the Bus Works to have its rear axle cooling system inspected. The bus then returned south without seeing service in Glasgow.

1972 was to be a significant year in the history of the Glasgow Atlantean, for in that year GCT got a new Chief Engineer, Alan Westwell. He had started as an apprentice at Liverpool Corporation and whilst working his way up the ladder had gained professional engineering qualifications. By the time he arrived in Glasgow he had worked with several English municipal operators, but his experience with Liverpool Corporation was vital as that concern had significant trouble with hot axles on its Atlanteans. However in 1972 the situation on Glasgow's Atlanteans was much more serious and defects were common in all the main systems within the bus, not to mention corrosion of parts of the body structure that were requiring immediate attention. Already in this chapter various alterations that were carried out on the Atlantean by GCT have been noted, but this failed to cure the most serious problem, overheating.

Until this time there had been tinkering with the problem, mainly by putting extra air vents in the rear engine cover. However Alan Westwell went for a radical solution to the problem. He set about personally inspecting the fleet, concentrating on the systems most prone to defect and just as importantly he set about reviewing the cause and rate of defection in GCT`s Atlanteans from official records. After this review, Mr Westwell concluded that the areas on the Atlantean that required attention were as follows:- automatic lubrication on the chassis, oil circuit filters, electrical units, transmission, air systems, the door control systems and water circuits. This last area poses an interesting dilemma. Water is both a friend and a foe of the engineer and as the following paragraphs illustrate, it was central to the problems under the bonnet in the PDR Atlanteans.

Water's usefulness is apparent in its ability to take heat away from the engine and thus prevent overheating. However in an operating environment like an engine, water is always looking for the easiest escape route. If there is a hole, even a tiny one, in the system then water will find it and then the problems really begin. It was clear the Chief Engineer had a battle on his hands to improve the availability of the PDR Atlantean fleet and with a battlefield mentality, he set about preparing the tactics his mechanics were to employ in order to defeat these problems.

The first strategy was to eliminate selected weak points in each of the above operating systems and once improved

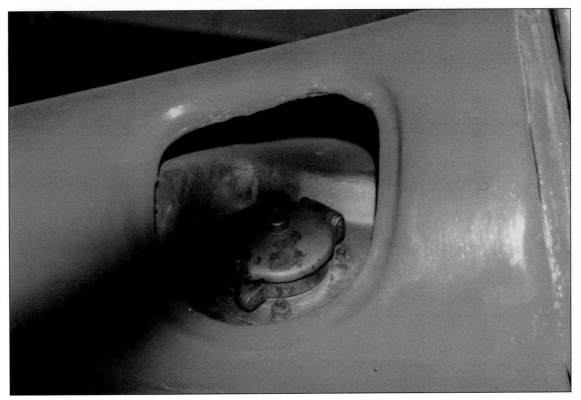

The above image shows the recessed water pipe for filing the radiator on LA 320. The image of LA 284 on the rear cover indicates that when new these buses also had a flap over this cap. (Author)

performance was attained, to begin a strategy of preventative maintenance with long term improved performance the goal.

Remedial action started by extending the water filling pipe for the radiator to the edge of the engine cover to allow easier filling of the radiator. Mr Westwell also found that the radiator caps themselves were contributing to the overheating problems. At its simplest, this was because the radiator caps were screwed on and off; if a driver or mechanic failed to fit the cap properly it was possible for the vibrations of the bus to shake the cap loose. The solution to this was the fitting of chains to all radiator caps to prevent their loss if they became loose. However, the radiator cap also served a more important function. When the coolant in the radiator heats up, the cap acts as a stopper and directs the hot water vapour through valves into the expansion chamber and subsequently on contraction back into the radiator circuit. It was discovered that the seals on the Atlantean radiator caps were not up to standard and a proper seal was acquired. Instructions were also sent out to night staff stating the importance of adequately and correctly filling the radiator as well as correctly fastening the radiator cap.

The hoses that carried water on its circuit of the engine were also causing concern. Mr Westwell had found that the hoses were becoming damaged through contact with other components under the bonnet and also through their location in a heated environment. In addition the jubilee clips holding the hoses in place were not providing adequate tension. In response to these problems a stock of good quality hoses were purchased. When an Atlantean became due for an MOT or was to have a new or reconditioned engine fitted, ALL its hoses were changed. Whilst this policy was not cheap, it was tiny compared to the cost of fitting a replacement engine. This action not only prevented leaks from occurring, but it also helped in reducing the overheating of engines.

As with the hoses, a better standard of fan belt was bought for the Atlanteans in order to avoid the stretching of belts which in turn led to the fan belt coming off its runners. Once again the policy of preventative maintenance was employed with the fan belts being changed on a regular basis rather than waiting for a failure. The reason for this was to prevent a water pump failure which would occur if the fan belts failed. This, of course, would mean that water wasn't circulating around the engine block, leading to overheating of the engine. The water pumps were also removed and overhauled as part of the drive for improved performance. There is a recurring theme to these defects, have you noticed it yet?

Other areas in the bus were also undergoing modifications. Mr Westwell had the automatic lubricant systems removed and replaced with manual grease nipples. A hardcore of handymen greasers were then trained in the correct procedures to employ so as to ensure the job was done correctly and to help reduce problems associated with wear. A torn or cracked cylinder head gasket allowed water to be lost as well as allowing the injectors to pump fuel oil into the engine. Oil was also getting onto the compressors and wiring which then carboned up. Therefore it was

imperative to find these defects early as part of the plan to improve reliability. Oil pumps didn't escape Mr Westwell's attention either. An immediate campaign was the renewal of oil filters and once improved reliability was attained, both the oil pumps and oil filters were changed on a regular basis to prevent failure of these units. The oil itself was changed, an improved quality was used which had a noticeable effect on increasing engine life. Finally, the wiring within the engine compartment was placed in non burn piping to protect it from the heat in the compartment and in the fuse box behind the driver's seat, fuses were replaced by circuit breakers.

A lot of work went into both the preparation and implantation of Alan Westwell's plan to improve the reliability of the Atlantean. The aforementioned modifications, both on their own and as part of the bigger picture, helped to increase the availability of the PDR Atlantean, as did the mechanics who suddenly had to change the way that they serviced the buses. But an even more radical modification for some of the PDR fleet almost became a reality.

The PTE hadn't just inherited a bus fleet from GCT, they inherited a fleet that was falling to bits, often literally. The half cabs that had been purchased between 1959 and 1961 to see off the majority of the trams hadn't stood up to the rigours of operation in Glasgow very well and this is reflected in the fact that the PTE inherited 1317 buses from GCT in June 1973, but just over 90 of these buses were classified as withdrawn. By May 1974 the fleet was down to 1281 buses, but 560 buses first registered before June 1963 remained on the fleet strength. The infamous graveyard at Knightswood Garage was becoming home to large numbers of these vehicles in a fleet which was reliant on large numbers of half cabs, some dating back to 1957 to hold the service network together. With the PVR significantly lower than the total number of buses owned, this meant some of the vehicles in the worst state could be cannibalised to maintain the serviceable buses. This, however, could only be a short tem solution, what was really needed was new buses. By May 1974 120 new vehicles had entered the fleet, but this was only around a tenth of the fleet strength and with a large fleet of elderly buses that it was desperate to get rid of, the PTE found itself in something of a quandary. The PTE ordered new buses, but Leyland weren't able to sate the PTE's demand and even if they had the new vehicles weren't going to appear overnight. Short term fixes saw elderly delicensed Atlanteans being overhauled and returned to service, LA 15 being one such bus to undergo a major overhaul before being returned to service.

A more radical idea that was given serious consideration was the rebodying of around 100 elderly PDR Atlanteans due their 12 year overhaul. The buses in the best condition were to be withdrawn to allow their bodywork to be removed and the chassis were then to have been sent to Alexanders in Falkirk for rebodying with new AL bodies. Whilst this was happening it was also planned to overhaul the chassis of these buses. Unfortunately, the plan never saw fruition and significant numbers of PDR withdrawals started in 1975. By then the fleet strength was down to 1258 buses, but in the previous year just over 100 new Atlanteans had entered the fleet as well as the first 20 MCW Metropolitans and the three pre-production Ailsa Volvos. The influx of new vehicles over the next few years would see the mechanical standard of the fleet improve considerably and fleet totals continued to fall, the peak vehicle requirement in 1975/6 was 874 buses and just two years later it was down to 744 buses.

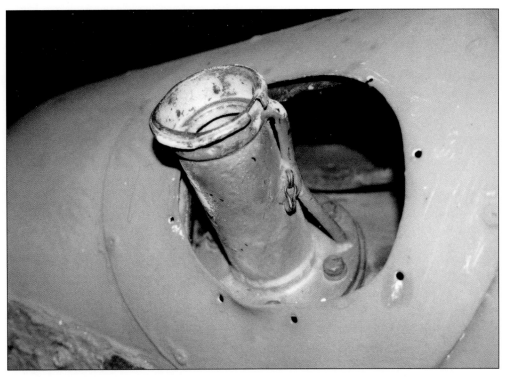

On the left is the water filling pipe for LA 389. The bolts holding the extended water pipe are visible as is the remains of the chain to hold the radiator cap in place. (Author)

The junction of Oswald Street and Argyle Street is the location of this rear end view of LA 211, below, in Carrick Furniture Store livery. The extended radiator filling pipe is clearly visible in this view as is the split rear upperdeck emergency door. (D.G. Wilson)

Security Screens

Violence against bus crews in Glasgow had been a long term problem and was not confined to adults, schoolbuses were a continual source of both violence against crews and vandalism of buses. Whilst initiatives like klaxons and radios were aids, they did not stop assaults on staff. The standard response from bus crews was to withdraw services from areas giving trouble until a suitable solution could be found. Violence against crews between Rutherglen and Castlemilk in May 1977 had led to a curfew being imposed on services 18/22 and 46 at weekends. Do not view these shenanigans as drunken high spirits, in one instance a driver was slashed and robbed of his takings. The only drawback with curfews is that they hit the law abiding citizens hardest, however, crews at Gartcraig Garage called of their curfew of Castlemilk after the PTE proposed a resolution of the issue. Usually, these solutions tended to work only in the short term and before long trouble would reappear, but this time the PTE proposed to fit 100 buses with a toughened safety screen to the cab doors of buses. If successful, the PTE would have the screens fitted to the rest of the fleet.

Attempts to find a more permanent solution to bus crew violence had begun in May 1975 when LA 630 was fitted as a test bus for anti vandal screens. The screen fitted to this bus was made from wire mesh and several different types of screen; some homemade and some from companies hoping to secure future orders from the PTE, were trialled before a successful design was found. The successful design was made locally in polycarbonate to a novel design. It was claimed that the screen was very resistant once sprayed and a bottle or hatchet would only crack the screen.

The value of the screens to both the PTE and drivers was proved in June 1977 when assaults on staff in Drumchapel led to evening services being suspended. The PTE`s response was to transfer 11 Atlanteans that already had screens fitted to Knightswood Garage. With LA 643/85/91/5/736/47/59/75/9/804/813 reallocated, services 9/19 and 20 soon had their evening services restored.

Crews operating buses without security screens continued to be attacked and after further protests from crews, the PTE decided to spend £ 100 000 installing screens to all of the bus fleet as previously promised. From mid October 1977 it was anticipated that 40 buses per week would be fitted and 300 screens had been fitted to buses by the end of March 1978. Clearly the success of the screens was passing around the bus industry as LA 1436, then new, visited Yorkshire Traction on the 24/5th February 1981 to allow its security screen to be inspected.

The security screen fitted to LA 1443 above, has small holes to allow communication between driver and passengers, but physical contact between the two is prevented. (Author)

Panoramic Glasgow

When Ronald Cox became the first Director General of the PTE, he decided that future orders of Atlanteans for the PTE should come with Alexander's Edinburgh style wide bay panoramic bodywork. This style of bodywork was familiar to Mr Cox as all of Edinburgh Atlanteans, bar an early handful, had carried this style of bodywork. The increased use of glass within the bodywork improved the appearance of an already attractive design and with less body pillars, improved the view out of the bus. However, replacing a metal component with one like glass, which has a lower tensile strength, has the potential for disaster written all over it. But that wasn't a concern for Mr Cox `s PTE who felt that the arrival of new buses and their increased reliability was something to tell the world about. The following paragraph appeared in the 1975/6 GGPTE annual report and with the benefit of hindsight brings a wry smile to the face, ` After some considerable problems with earlier models of this vehicle (PDR Atlanteans), those delivered during the last four to five years (late PDR / early AN 68 Atlanteans) have become increasingly reliable with a consequent reduction in service disruption.` The irony in this statement is that some of the buses they are praising

are those delivered from January 1974, i.e. LA 751 onwards, with panoramic bodies. It is easy with hindsight to castigate the PTE and say that perhaps they should have done some things differently, but it has to be remembered that the PTE inherited a bus fleet from GCT with reliability problems so bodywork problems with new, serviceable buses, were hardly a concern when the service network was in a state of collapse because not enough of the old buses worked. But bodywork problems there were and as the old adage says, `never put off a job till tomorrow that can be done today,` and the PTE even got advance notice of what was in store for their panoramic Atlanteans.

Renfrewshire independent operator Mc Gills of Barrhead had purchased two Daimler Fleetlines, XHS 923/4H, with Edinburgh style dual door Alexander panoramic bodies in 1969/70. By 1976 Mc Gills had decided to convert both vehicles to single door and insert extra window pillars in the lower saloon. The reason for this was that Mc Gills felt that the long bays of the panoramic windows were not as secure on the Fleetline chassis as they should have been. The reason that these buses are important to Glasgow is that because of other work requiring to be done by

Panoramic bodied Atlantean, LA 926 is seen at the Larkfield Open Day in April 1978. The raised caps just below the `Slix` advert are pipe drain covers. These were added to post LA 751 Atlanteans to allow surplus water from cleaning and also rain ingress from poor fitting windows, to drain away from the upper deck. (D. Cousins)

Mc Gills, 923 was towed to Larkfield Bus Works for the remedial work to be undertaken. If the Mc Gills buses were the foghorn, then the PTE was the ship heading towards the rocks. Unfortunately, for the PTE, their former Chief Engineer and the man who would have recognised what Mc Gills were doing, was 85 miles to the north east of Glasgow having taken up the post of Director of Public Transport for Tayside Region in 1975.

Prior to the first Atlantean with panoramic bodywork arriving in Glasgow, Alan Westwell was already worried by the lack of support within the Edinburgh wide bay bodywork. He had identified two key areas of weakness within the design. Putting two large apertures into a bus body, namely the entrance and exit doors, places stress on the bus framework that can only be successfully dealt with if this stress can be distributed throughout the rest of the framework. On the panoramic bodied Atlantean this did not occur and this was the second weakness that the Chief Engineer had identified. The body framework consisted of vertical pillars that were mounted on chassis outriggers. A vertical pillar starting on the offside chassis outrigger should continue up and over the roof before finishing attached to the nearside chassis outrigger directly opposite its starting point. This process should be repeated at every chassis outrigger and effectively formed a series of hoops down the length of the unbuilt chassis to give stability and rigidity to the framework. In effect every window pillar is a vertical pillar of the framework. On Edinburgh's Atlanteans, Mr Cox had stated that the vertical pillars should always be in line. This meant that some vertical pillars existed, but were

unable to complete their loop of the bus as they would have dissected a window pane on one side of the body, i.e. the wide bay arrangement led to some vertical pillars failing to exist.

The first Director General of the PTE, Ronald Cox, had been more interested in the aesthetic appearance of the panoramic bodywork than the potential weaknesses within the body's design, but he wasn't the only one who failed to spot the weaknesses within the design. After Mr Cox retired in 1976, wide bay bodied Atlanteans kept being purchased by the PTE until the last, LA 1350, arrived in February 1980. Alan Westwell returned to the PTE in November 1979 as its third Director General and a change of body style was about to be implemented on the last 99 Atlanteans, LA 1351– 1449, that the PTE would purchase new. The oldest panoramic bodied Atlanteans were now 6 years old and were starting to show signs of structural problems that were directly related to the lack of rigidity within their framework. These weaknesses of design could be seen with cracking and corrosion affecting the framework below the lower deck floor between the staircase and the rear wheelarch. Despite the presence of these defects, Alexanders still needed to be sold on the importance of the vertical pillars joining the chassis outriggers, especially before and after each axle. Alan Westwell set about convincing the bodybuilder by inviting the company to a demonstration involving panoramic bodied Atlanteans. With their outer panels removed and the inner stress panels treated with a solution to highlight stress raisers, the buses were then run over railway sleepers

Two panoramic Atlanteans pass each other at the junction of Cambridge Street and Renfrew Street. This photo taken from the veranda of the former Grandfayre store shows how the window pillars line up on the nearside of the bus, but not on the offside. (David.G.Wilson)

in a yard. Immediately the stresses and fractures within the bodywork were visible for all to see.

Various attempts to solve the defects within the framework of these buses were initiated, starting with LA 795 in September 1980 which had two short bay windows inserted over the rear offside axle. More radical still was the rebuilding of LA 1180 and LA 1324 in March 1981 with short bays replacing the lower deck wide bay windows. LA 1330 was to follow shortly afterwards in May 1981. With both the cause and the visible proof of the defects now known, the repairs were actually straightforward. Strength and integrity had to be returned to the framework of the body, especially around the axles. By fitting short bay windows into the lower deck of these vehicles, a stiffer structure was produced and a complete pillar ring was made around the vehicles.

To allow the engineers to assess the success of these modifications under service conditions, LA 1324/1330 were filled with sand bags to simulate passenger weight and sent out on the city's streets operating a shadow timetable. The repairs were successful but effectively rebuilding an ageing bus, this wasn't just a modification, was both labour intensive and expensive and by late 1981 the PTE was no longer able to deny there were problems with its panoramic bodied Atlanteans. It admitted that body defects had been discovered in many of its 601 panoramic bodied Atlanteans, although the PTE was confident that repairs could be carried out. In an effort to solve the problem, modifications to reinforce the side frames were undertaken at both Larkfield Bus Works and

at the Alexanders factory in Falkirk. Some repairs were easier to spot than others. Over the next ten years around a dozen buses were rebuilt with short bay bodywork inserted on one, or both sides of the lower saloon. The majority of buses that were retained, however, were repaired with no external evidence that strengthening had taken place. Whichever sort of repair was carried out, wasn't cheap and at a time when the average life of a Glasgow bus was down to ten years it was regarded as more prudent to life extend some of the earliest short bay bodied AN 68 Atlanteans, namely LA 664/678/683 and buses between LA 700 and LA 750 than repair defective panoramic bodied examples. The last 99 Atlanteans, LA 1351– 1449 also received short bay bodywork, which from an engineering viewpoint, Alan Westwell had always preferred to the panoramic body. By April 1983 many panoramics that had not been repaired, mainly between LA 751 and LA 1050, had been withdrawn and whilst some of these buses were to find new owners willing to repair them, others went to the scrapyard or were broken up at the Bus Works. This latter fate included LA 767/833/42/986/1020. By April 1983 a large number of withdrawn panoramic bodied Atlanteans were in store and the decision was taken to repaint these buses all over green prior to sale.

In finishing this chapter it is worth mentioning the panoramic bodied Atlanteans in both the Edinburgh and the Tyne and Wear fleets. It has always been assumed that these buses didn't suffer from the problems that had afflicted the Glasgow examples. Possible reasons such as better road conditions and better driving being cited as possible

By November 2004 the long process of restoring LA 1324 to Strathclyde Transport livery had begun. In this view the short bay windows inserted into her lower decks are visible. (Author)

reasons. Whilst both of these factors will undoubtedly lengthen the career of any bus, it is doubtful from the facts presented in this chapter that either of these would have prevented the problems that occurred in Glasgow. Indeed, contrary to popular belief, the Edinburgh panoramic bodied Atlanteans suffered just as badly as the Glasgow ones, the only difference being that in Edinburgh the decision was taken to repair the fleet rather than dispose of it prematurely. Thus the Capital's Atlanteans were rebuilt without any visible signs of repair or strengthening. As with the Glasgow buses, the Atlanteans in Edinburgh suffered problems on the offside of the lower saloon and several preservationists with an interest in the Edinburgh bus scene, feel that the only batch of short bay bodied Atlanteans for Edinburgh, delivered in 1966, were the best

because they didn't develop the bodywork problems that beset every subsequent batch ordered thereafter.

Tyne and Wear ordered both standard length and longer length Atlanteans with the panoramic body. The shorter ones would have undoubtedly suffered the same problems as the Glasgow examples. The longer buses are more interesting. Disregarding the staircase, it didn't matter whether it was on the nearside or the offside of the chassis, the important thing on these buses are the window pillars. The longer length allowed an extra window pillar on each side of the chassis, but unlike the shorter length panoramics, all the pillars on the offside were directly opposite a pillar on the nearside. Whilst these vehicles were still not as secure as short bay bodied examples, they were more secure than the shorter length panoramic bodied Atlanteans.

Former Tyne and Wear Atlantean GLA 36 was one of the 33 feet long examples that operated for SBL and GCT. Compare the photos of the nearside, upper image, and the offside, lower image, and note the position of the window pillars compared to the Glasgow examples shown on pages 60 and 61. (Both B. Ridgway)

Centre door ? Whit centre doar?

The new PTE didn't share GCT's enthusiasm for dual door buses, deciding shortly after its formation to remove the centre door from dual door buses and to revert to single doors for future orders. This was probably a good thing as the Glasgow public, having mastered getting on at the front of the bus instead of the rear, were not taking to the idea that you could exit a bus from a different point to which one entered. Despite the public's misgivings about dual door buses, some drivers liked them. On cross city routes the second door could be used to allow alighting at busy stops in the city centre. The use of the second door wasn't confined to the city centre as there were busy stops all around the city at places like Bridgeton Cross and Partick, not to forget the many early morning workers' services and also any of the larger football grounds when a game was being played. The one surprise about the PTE's move to single door buses was that Mr Cox had seen the introduction of dual door buses to Edinburgh, and even to the last deliveries in 1981 only a small number of the Capital's Atlanteans were delivered in single door form.

The first Atlantean to PTE specifications, LA 751, arrived in November 1973 with a single door and it wasn't long until work started on removing the second door from dual door buses. In 1974 LAs 559/736 were the first buses to be treated and the only ones intentionally finished to H45/31F layout. The work involved not only removing the centre door, but also the bulkheads in the lower saloon around the former centre door platform. The other H45/31F conversion was LA 644, but as this was rebuilt after serious fire damage it doesn't count in the context of this chapter. With the exception of LA 570, the rest of the two door fleet that were treated were finished in H45/29F layout.

Originally, the PTE had planned to rebuild the Atlanteans in two stages at Larkfield Bus Works. The first stage would see the buses rebuilt to H45/27F layout with the centre doors still in situ. A luggage pen would be placed between the bulkheads in the lower saloon and the doors were to be panelled over on the outside up to window height. When the buses were due their overhaul, they would be rebuilt to H45/31F with the doorway removed and an extra window inserted. LA 570 emerged in 1974 as the only bus to be rebuilt to this first stage and was quickly moved on to the second stage by January 1975, but to H45/29F layout. LA 548 was also rebuilt to H45/29F layout, but retained the bulkheads in the lower saloon and had a bench seat for two people inserted across the former centre door platform. Externally, the bus was panelled over and an extra window inserted in place of the former centre door. This became the standard modification of two door Atlanteans until 1979 when the final examples were dealt with. The cost of rebuilding the buses in two stages and removing the former centre door bulkheads had been deemed excessive; so this led to the cheaper second method being used.

By late 1978 the remaining two door examples were all being used as single door buses, the centre door having been disconnected. The 35 buses involved being LA 653/5/7/60/2/4/8/80-4/94/5/7-9/713-5/7-21/3/ 8/30/ 4/737/8/41/2/4/5. The last two door buses were withdrawn in 1980 without being modified and these 14 buses were LA 681/4/5/9/713/4/7/8/20/8/30/5/7/8. As usual, some of the withdrawn buses ended up at the driving school and in November 1979 LA 682 appeared with its front door panelled over and replaced by a window, its centre door still in place. Ten Atlanteans, LA 680/2/97/8/700/10/19/41/2/5 were rebuilt in this manner for the driving school between 1979 and 1981 with buses classified as H—/—C layout.

The image, above left, shows in detail LA 708 in its original two door configuration. (David.G. Wilson)
On the right, is an image of LA 664 from June 1995 with its centre door removed, although the bulkheads for the former centre exit clearly remain. (B. Ridgway)

The Single Atlanteans

The first single deck Atlantean, SA 1, appeared in June 1982 and over the following 26 months another seven of these vehicles would take to the roads, all based on standard panoramic double deck Atlanteans. The work to convert these buses was undertaken at Larkfield Bus Works and merely emphasises the skill of the staff employed there. Besides removing the upper deck and the rear engine shrouds, the stairwell over the front offside axle was removed, the early panoramic windows with sliders were replaced by 'Young's' type hopper windows and a new roof with small front and rear overhangs was constructed. Reflecting the buses initial allocation to city centre shuttle work the seating capacity of the conversions up to SA 6 remained unchanged from their previous lower saloon capacities of 31 seats. All the conversions were finished in all over Strathclyde red with black window surrounds and black skirt, although SA 1 would later be repainted as an all over advert for Stakis Hotels. SA 1 was put to work on the inter station service 98, Central Station to Queen Street Station, that had seen many small and wonderful vehicles employed on it, the Seddon midi buses, the lone Bedford coach and less gloriously the Leyland Nationals. SA 2/3 arrived in July 1982 and soon were at work alongside SA 1 on the 98.

The following March saw the arrival of SA 4/5 with both buses being allocated to Knightswood Garage for use on the Drumchapel Interlink service 96. Previously operated by double deck Atlanteans, the service connected the various outlying parts of this large overspill estate in the North West of the city with the railway station where a frequent electric train service could take passengers east to the city centre or west to Balloch or Helensburgh. SA6 arrived in November 1983 and is believed to have been selected as a result of a low bridge collision. There is a picture of a decapitated LA 1117 at Larkfield Garage elsewhere in this book. The bus was sent almost immediately to Millport Motors after its conversion and it remained there until April 1984. The final SA Atlanteans were SA 7/8 which arrived in August 1984 and differed from the rest of the class in having 35 seats, the extra 4 seats being inserted over the front offside wheel arch.

The buses remained in service until November 1988 when SA 1- 3 and SA 5- 7 were withdrawn and the two remaining examples were transferred from Knightswood Garage to Possilpark Garage where they stayed in service for another four months. The buses were sold to dealer, Sykes of Barnsley, and as far as can be ascertained most of these vehicles met their end, although SA 6 was rumoured to have found further use after leaving Glasgow, but has since disappeared.

Besides Knightswood and Larkfield Garages, which

also used the SAs on service 85 to Rutherglen and Spittal, the buses also saw use from Parkhead and Possilpark Garages. Parkhead used them on service 13, City Centre to Parkhead, and Possilpark put them to work on service 43, Ruchill to Summerston.

As with other midibuses operated by the PTE in the early eighties, these vehicles found themselves sent throughout Strathclyde Region to aid small operators with vehicle shortages. Besides SA 6 mentioned above, SA 1 was loaned to Mc Nair of Girvan from November 1983 to February 1984 when it was replaced by SA 3 which also stayed three months until May that year. SA 2 went on long term loan with Millport Motors from July 1983 until January 1984.

A lot of time, effort and money went into the conversion of these vehicles and with operational lives of between four and six and a half years the success of these vehicles is questionable. By today's standards these midibuses were heavier, noisier and had a larger engine than a Dennis Dart or an Optare Solo, but it should not be forgotten that had the problem with the panoramic bodies not reared its head, it is doubtful whether any single deck Atlanteans would have appeared. With the exception of one bus, LA 1117 , converted as a result of a bridge strike, all the SAs came from the batches, LA 751– 1050, which saw the least number of repairs to their defective panoramic bodies and the highest number of disposals.

The PTE was on the lookout for a small bus and had tried a selection of small vehicles including Seddons and Leyland Nationals with only mixed success in the late seventies and early eighties, so there was a niche in the market waiting to be found and Dennis was still to notice it. There were also mechanical advantages of using cut down Atlanteans. In the eighties the Atlantean was considered to be a low floor chassis and therefore it was suitable for working on routes where, for various reasons, passengers might have boarding difficulties. The cut down Atlanteans also needed the same spare parts as the big bus Atlanteans, so a separate stock of spare parts didn't need to be acquired and rotated round garages when reallocation occurred. To buy a bus that specifically suited one route meant it wouldn't necessarily be adaptable for use at other garages, whereas the Atlanteans were adaptable to operate a wide variety of routes, including big bus routes if needed.

Including their period of service as double deckers, the SAs managed between 12 and 14 years service for Strathclyde PTE/ Buses which would be about average for most buses built in the mid seventies anyway. What really finished the buses off was MCW bringing its Metrorider minibus to the deregulated bus market in 1987. Here for the first time was a minibus specifically built for use by the bus industry as a small bus and operators throughout

LA188 is seen, above, in her new surroundings in New South Wales, Australia. THe fitting of grilles to the front of the bus by her owner is clearly evident. However an extra indicator has been added above the entrance doors and the side drirection indicator has been relocated below the windscreen on the front dash. (A Potts)

PTE liveried LA 341, above, and LA 381, wearing her first AOA for Transcard, wait for a green light in George Square. On the other side of the road the rear of LA 617 drives off into the distance. (David G. Wilson)

Top image finds GLA 664 heading for the SECC in June 1995. The decals on either side of the destination screen highlight the centenary in 1994 of public transport in Glasgow. (B. Ridgway)

Lower image finds LA 680 passing Buchannan Bus Station on driver training duties. The removal of the front entrance gives the bus an unbalanced look. Despite the upper deck of the later training buses being sealed off, they retained their seats! (Billy Nicol)

LA 944 travels east long Renfrew Street, her Young's hoppers just being visible. (David G. Wilson)

LA 1028, above, was unique in the fleet by virtue of having her demister motors above rather than below the windscreen. Despite lasting until 1983, this bus only wore PTE 1 livery. (David G. Wilson)

The yellow ` Exact Fare` viynls were not used for long on PTE 4 liveried buses. LA 776, above, in Bath Street was one bus to be treated in this manner. Note the early Strathclyde Transport fleetname. (David G. Wilson)

LA 1218 operated in passenger service whilst in the disguise that she wore in the film `Carla's Song`
All reference to Strathclyde Buses being obliterated by the ` No Smoking ` advertisements. (Billy Nicol)

Top Image:- LA 826 found use with the Education Department of Strathclyde Regional Council after being withdrawn by the PTE. Here she is seen parked on an Industrial Estate at Shawfield in 2005. (Author)

Lower Image:- LA 975 was used as a survey bus by the PTE. The work to refit the bus being undertaken at Larkfield Bus Works. Here she is seen in Saint Enoch Square. (David G. Wilson)

LA 1326, above, undergoes a partial repaint at Larkfield Bus Works from PTE 1 to PTE 3 livery. (David G. Wilson)

*LA 1332, below, sits in Clydebank Bus Station on a dank and dismal West of Scotland day. The reversed
LA 751 type of destination display and earlier style of front panel are evident. (Billy Nicol)*

The top image sees LA 729 lead a line of Atlanteans of different liveries and body styles down Renfield Street passed the former Corporation Head Office on the corner of Bath Street. (David G. Wilson)

LA 1379, right, has a short lived variant of the `Exact Fare` vinyl used on the front of buses. Just visible is the early Strathclyde Transport fleetname. (David G. Wilson)

72

LA 957, top, is seen in George Square carrying the 1978 City Tour livery. (David G. Wilson)

LA 963, bottom, was also in George Square , this time in 1996 operating the City Tour on behalf of Guide Friday.
Beside the loss of its roof, the bus has also lost its original front panel and its engine shrouds. (Billy Nicol)

LA 1266, above, was one of five buses from the FSU/T batch to carry an allover advert. Note how the `Exact Fare` stickers have been applied to the windscreen due to the advert on the front panel. (David G,. Wilson)

LA 1411, above, was one of only a small number of Atlanteans to carry a broadside advert. Here she is passing the now demolished Apollo Theatre in Renfield Street in 1984. Note the complete absence of black paint on this bus. (David G. Wilson)

PTE 2 liveried LA 1427, above, is seen in Saint Enoch Square early in its career. The white area behind the driver's cab indicates that this bus was painted when new at Alexanders in Falkirk. (David G Wilson)

LA 1427, above, met its end when it was deroofed on a rail replacement service at Carntyne Station on Christmas Eve 1995. By the following May the bus was lying inside Larkfield. The bus displays evidence of cannibalisation having started. (Billy Nicol)

LA 947, top, displays the unique and less than inspiring version of PTE 3 livery worn by this bus. (David G. Wilson)

Coach liveried LA 1402, lower image, sits in Saint Enoch Bus Station. To describe these buses as coaches really was pushing their credibility too far. Their public address systems and livery apart, LA 1401/2/19, were bog standard members of the LA 1351– 1449 batch. (Billy Nicol)

Top Image:- Govan Bus Station in August 1993 and three former Busways Atlanteans layover. Nearest the camera is GLA 31 in the intermediate GCT/SBL livery that some GCT vehicles wore for a few months after GCT began operations. (David G Wilson)

Lower Image:- LA 1367 and LA 1233 provide an interesting comparison as they sit at traffic lights in Jamaica Street with Midland Street. The higher driving position of LA 1367 being evident. (B. Ridgway)

Top Image:- C 935 is seen when on hire to Strathclyde Buses from Busways in the aftermath of the Larkfield Garage fire in 1992. After being bought by SBL the bus became LA 1465. (David G. Wilson)

Lower Image:- Seen at Kelvingrove is Park Royal bodied C 918. Although on hire to SBL from Western Scottish, this bus had been new to Greater Manchester Transport. (Billy Nicol)

Complementing the offside view of GLA 6 on page 108 is this nearside view of the same bus, note the front door arrangement of these buses. In this view the bus is on loan to Strathclyde Buses.(B. Ridgway)

KCB 1923, one time GGPTE LA 1052, departs Buchannan Bus Station for Drumchapel in June 1995. (B. Ridgway)

Top Image:- Nothing highlights the sadness of scrapyards more than when you find a bus you recall as a bright, dry and mobile piece of machinery lying as a rusting hulk awaiting its end. One time Silver Jubilee Atlantean LA 1135, and later GLA 58, waits to be torn apart by the mechanical grab at Dunmore's in February 2005. (Author)

Lower Image:- LA 1423 lies inside Larkfield Garage in May 1996 after having been withdrawn due to an electrical fault whilst in service in East Kilbride. (Billy Nicol)

LA 708, top image, was one of only a small number of Atlanteans with engine shrouds to be delivered to the PTE in GCT livery. This bus was rebuilt to single door layout during 1977. (David G Wilson)

LA 820, lower image, is seen in Union Street, note the non standard application of black paint above the front windscreen. Following behind is an LA 61x carrying a more standard version of PTE 3 livery. (David G. Wilson)

Britain bought them. SBL bought a large number of them during 1987/8 and these purchases spelt the end for the SAs. It is interesting to note that when the SAs were being created, 84 short bay AN 68s between LA 601 and LA 750 were withdrawn between 1982 and 1984 with none being rebuilt to single deck. You just wonder what a single deck LA 6xx would have looked like, don't you?

Below is a table listing the details of the SA Atlanteans.

New Fleet No.	Old Fleet No.	Registration No.	Date of Conversion	Date of Withdrawal	Capacity
SA 1	LA 850	SGA 733N	6/82	11/88	B 31F
SA 2	LA 930	JUS 777N	7/82	11/88	B 31F
SA 3	LA 962	KSU 838P	7/82	11/88	B 31F
SA 4	LA 871	GNS 663N	3/83	3/89	B 31F
SA 5	LA 979	KSU 855P	3/83	11/88	B 31F
SA 6	LA 1117	TGE 836R	11/83	11/88	B 31F
SA 7	LA 918	JGA 200N	8/84	11/88	B 35F
SA 8	LA 938	JUS 785N	8/84	3/89	B 35F

A rear end profile of SA 1 at Queen Street Station reveals not only the rebuilt back end, but also the extra window inserted over the front offside axle. (A. Douglas)

SA 3 is seen on a local circular shoppers service in Rutherglen (A. Douglas)

 # City Tours

Glasgow Corporation had operated tours of Glasgow prior to the second world war, but had ignored this market in the post war period. By the seventies the Scottish Bus Group was servicing the Glasgow City Tour market through its Alexander (Midland) subsidiary. The 800th anniversary of burgh status being bestowed upon Glasgow was an ideal excuse for the PTE to commence operation of a city tour. In connection with the anniversary, a Glasgow 800 festival was also staged and the PTE took the opportunity to display a selection of vehicles from 1894 to 1975.

Initially, the tour was to run for just four weeks from the middle of April 1975 and would consist of a 90 minute tour passing buildings of architectural or historical interest within the city for a flat fare of 30 pence. To operate the tour two freshly overhauled Atlanteans, LA 418/32, were chosen and the buses were painted in special Glasgow 800 liveries, yellow on LA 418 and white on LA 432. To allow special taped commentaries to be used during the tour, the buses had public address, (p.a.), systems fitted, a feature that subsequently became standard on all the City Tour Atlanteans. The tour soon proved to be more popular than predicted and it was soon extended to the end of September, attracting both Glaswegians and tourists alike. This popularity soon led to standard liveried LA 416 being fitted with a p.a. system to allow it to be used as a back up vehicle. In the first season of the tour around 44 000 passengers were carried and it was reckoned that around half of this number were visitors to the city. The tour ceased as planned on the 29th September, but before the buses were returned to normal duties they were used to operate special tours of the route for schools. During October the p.a. systems were removed and the buses returned to passenger service from Larkfield Garage carrying 800 livery, which would last another month before the buses were repainted into GGPTE livery.

No doubt buoyed by the success of the previous year, the tour returned in 1976 using three recently delivered Atlanteans, LA 1000/22/30, which were fitted with p.a. systems for the tour. Once again each bus wore its own version of tour livery, yellow on LA 1000, white on LA 1022 and green on LA 1030 with the logo, ` City Bus Tour` being common to each vehicle. The tour started on the 16th April, however the Bus Group, no doubt worried of the effect on its City Tour, tried unsuccessfully to place an objection. By the middle of May standard liveried LA 914 had been moved to Parkhead Garage to act as a back up vehicle and by the end of the season 22 000 passengers had been carried, a sharp contrast on the previous season. Once again special tours were operated for schools prior to the buses involved being returned to normal duties and repaint to PTE livery.

The Queen's Silver Jubilee arrived in 1977 and the PTE got into the spirit by repainting seven Atlanteans LA 1130– 5/42, in a special livery of all over silver with sky blue waistband. Only LA 1130– 3 were chosen to operate the city tour and once again p.a systems and signwriting were added prior to the tour commencing, an interesting development being the use of conductors as couriers on the buses. A fourth Atlantean, LA 1134, had the p.a. system fitted but no signwrting so that it could be used as a back up vehicle on the 1977 tour. Two tours were operated that year, the main tour, now with an 80 pence fare, was operated by Possilpark Garage and had been revised slightly with new attractions like the Clyde Tunnel and parts of the M8 motorway added to the itinerary. The PTE also decided to introduce a shorter Old Glasgow Tour which was one man operated using buses and crews from Langside Garage. Operating every afternoon, the shorter tour visited the People's Palace, Glasgow Cathedral, Provand`s Lordship and the Museum of Transport.

By now the tour concept was established and settled down to carry around 15 000 passengers per season. In 1978, the tour was operating out of Gartcraig Garage and LA 1130– 2/4 were painted in a pink and white scheme, the third livery in less than a year for these buses. Having lost their Silver Jubilee scheme for PTE colours in November 1977, they were repainted in the 1978 tour scheme in the spring of 1978 and for a few weeks at the start of the tour both LA 1133 and LA 1134 operated the tour in PTE 1 livery. A new addition for the 1978 tour was LA 957 which had recently been converted to open top after sustaining accident damage. The PTE clearly feeling that when the clouds weren't dropping copious amounts of convected Atlantic Ocean on Glasgow and the wind wasn't blowing down from the Artic, that Glaswegians might enjoy seeing the city's attractions without the roof getting in the way. 1979 saw LA 957 joined by LA 1262/3/4 on the tour with an all over white livery and blue signwriting being used. As in previous years, LA 1262/3/4 were repainted into PTE livery during November or December and LA 1262/3 rejoined LA 957 for the 1980 tour in a white and ochre scheme.

Recently delivered LA 1401/2 were repainted into the white and ochre scheme for the 1981 tour, but wore a livery variation in having black instead of ochre bumpers. During the 1981/2 close season both buses saw use on normal duties whilst still carrying city tour livery. The buses carried this livery until 1984 when along with LA 957 and LA 1220, they received the white/orange and black livery that became synonymous with the PTE`s coach fleet. After LA 1401 was written off in October 1985, LA 1419 was fitted with p.a. systems and painted in the coach livery as its replacement. With the disposal of LA 957/1220 in 1988, the only Atlanteans left in coach livery were LA 1402/19 which they carried until the end of 1990 when both vehicles gained standard SBL orange/black livery. LA 1402 is noteworthy in that it spent around nine and a half years out of fleet livery, the longest time out of fleet livery for any Glasgow Atlantean.

LA 1130 traverses Clyde Street, close to the junction with Jamaica Street, whilst undertaking a journey in the 1978 tour programme. (D. Cousins)

LA 1262 is on the north side of George Square carrying the 1979 tour livery. Compared with previous years this livery lacked verve and imagination. Note the larger driver's cab window. (David.G Wilson)

Atlantean Away Days

As is well known, the early Glasgow Atlanteans, LA 6/83/91/138, were sent on loan to other operators to extol the virtues of the chassis. Not so well known are the later Atlanteans that were sent to help operators in times of trouble. GGPTE set the ball rolling when a quartet of Atlanteans, LA 744/ 1136/61/1235, headed north to Grampian Regional Transport in May 1978, LA 1235 was notable in having only entered service with the PTE the previous month. LA 744 was in Aberdeen as part of the exchange of vehicles that had brought GRT Leyland National 70 to Glasgow to demonstrate the National's qualities and would stay in the granite city until the following March, gaining local fleetnumber 333. The other three buses were covering a vehicle shortage in Aberdeen and LA 1136/61/1235 gained local fleetnumbers 336/4/5 respectively during their two month stay.

The PTE`s Atlanteans were in demand during May 78 with a quintet of buses, LA 1162/1219/21/9/36 going on loan to Central SMT. A shortage of useable buses and delays to its next order of Alexander `y` type Leyland Leopards had left Central needing to borrow buses. The Atlanteans were sent to Airbles Garage, Motherwell, and put to work on services 64/6 which ran from Glasgow to West Crindledyke. All of the buses had seen little service in Glasgow and it is rumoured that one bus, (LA 1236 is most likely), was sent to Motherwell before being used by the PTE. By the end of the month only LA 1162 remained in Lanarkshire and within a few weeks it had followed the others back to Glasgow. The Atlanteans must have provided an interesting contrast to the public with Central's bog standard high floor Leyland Leopards and elderly low floor Bristol Lodekkas. Besides the height of the seating above the road, the Leopards also had a very narrow entrance, neither of which applied to the Atlantean. One wonders what the drivers at Airbles made of the on loan buses. The Lodekkas for all their great qualities required the driver to sit next to a Gardner engine for the shift and the Leopards had double de-clutch crash gearboxes on the first to second gearchange. From personal experience, using a crash gearbox on a heavily used route is both tiring and physical. The Atlanteans with their semi automatic gearboxes and the engine at the rear of the bus, must have caught a few drivers eyes.

Over a two year period starting in June 1979, Grahams of Paisley borrowed a number of PTE Atlanteans. The loans began when vehicle shortages required LA 402/53 to be sent to Paisley. Although both buses were returned to the PTE unused. LA 1029 was borrowed for a month from January to February 1980 before LA 668 replaced it. By May LA 1163/4/1200 were in Paisley, but LA 1163/1200 were back with the PTE by the middle of May with LA 1238 replacing LA 1200. Both LA 1164 and LA 1238 remained

at Grahams for two months with LA 1238 being the last of the four buses to return to Glasgow. A final loan to this popular Renfrewshire operator occurred in February 1981 when LA 642 made the trip down the M8, the same month that new Atlantean LA 1436 was being inspected at Yorkshire Traction. Apart from the loans involving the single deck Atlanteans, loans died out through the rest of the eighties. Deregulation almost certainly played a part as operators refrained from buying new buses which meant no spare withdrawn buses to hire out and in any case most fleets had been reduced to the smallest number required to be operational.

An unusual event in 1989 saw 20 Atlanteans, LA 1251/3/5/7/8/60– 3/5/73– 5/81– 3/96/1306/7/19, sold by accident to Sheffield based dealer Johnson's. Confusion surrounds the whole episode and whilst it was reported that the buses travelled south, some SBL drivers at the time contradict this stating that none of the buses ever left service and that the whole thing was an error in the administration department. Nonetheless, once the error was discovered the buses were soon returned to SBL ownership and all kept running until 1997 when mass withdrawal of Atlanteans began as First Group started modernising its Glasgow subsidiary.

By the mid– nineties with the Strathclyde Buses Group owning GCT, KCB and SBL, loans and swaps between these three companies were taking place at a tremendous pace and these are covered in more detail in the relevant chapters dealing with GCT and KCB. By 1997 the Atlantean was on the way out in Glasgow and in early November LA 1362/5 were sent on loan within First Bus to Midland Bluebird for a fortnight. Second-hand Atlantean LA 547 was sent to Midland's Larbert Road Garage in January 1998 and two months later, LA 539/49 were operating out of Linlithgow Garage as 758/9 with Midland acquiring both of these vehicles the following month . Resident Atlanteans LA 1371/1442 were also sent on loan to Midland in early 1998 and gained fleetnumbers 777/8 during their stay. With about 70 Atlanteans left in service with First Glasgow, LA 1371 was withdrawn on its return from Midland. However doubt surrounds its exact demise. It may have gone direct from Livingston Garage to Dunmore's in Larkhall for scrap or it may have been sent to the closed Old Kilpatrick Garage for storage prior to being sent to Dunmore's. The only certainty is that it didn't return to service in Glasgow. LA 1442 was to be sold to Glasgow preservationist Michael Roulston and in its distressed state was to become familiar to members of the Glasgow Bus Museum over the next few years. The bus was finally sold to Dunmore's for scrap in late 2003, but not before Mark Budd, owner of LA 1443, and myself, had managed to secure a large upper deck laminate panel and some other parts for his bus.

A rainy day in September 1978 finds LA 744 in Aberdeen, just visible in the corner of the windscreen is a paper label with the bus`s Grampian fleetnumber `333`. (D. Cousins)

A shiny LA 1236 complete with a typical Scottish Bus Group plethora of paper stickers operates a 201 journey for Central SMT. (A.J. Douglas).

All Over Advertisements

The All Over Advertisement bus, AOA, was a common site in Glasgow from the early seventies until the late nineties when they all but vanished from Glasgow's streets. Whilst some people viewed these moving billboards as hideous, others enjoyed the vivid colours and elaborate designs that all their jiggery pokery brought to the city's streets. It is pleasing to record that in recent years the AOA bus has made a comeback within Glasgow; however, it must be remembered that plastering adverts all over a bus isn't done to brighten up dull days, but for financial purposes. Wonga talks people, love it or loath it; money does indeed make the world go round! Do you think there would be any AOA buses if they didn't `maximise the revenue potential` of bus operators? Of course not, and if you are running a fleet that is loosing money, as GCT`s was in the seventies, then you would consider anything to raise extra cash. Those outside the bus industry possibly don't realise the amount of scheduling that is involved in bus operations. Not only are buses allocated to routes for reasons of length, height, seating capacity, weight etc, but they are also allocated to specific schedules within a route. Not much point having your highest capacity buses at the suburban end of a route just as the evening rush hour hits full flow, is there? It follows therefore that an AOA bus will be allocated to a route with a high potential viewing audience. Not only that,

the bus will be allocated to a duty that allows the maximum number of hours on that route. In the following chapter I intend to show, as far as possible, the routes, garages and dates that particular Atlanteans spent carrying individual liveries. It is interesting to note how many of those early GCT or GGPTE advertising routes are now part of First Glasgow's Overground network.

The first bus in Scotland to receive an All Over Advert was LA 230 in March 1972 when it received an advert for Barclaycard. The sixty second and last Glasgow Atlantean to receive an AOA was LA 1426 in May 1990 for the BP Dome of Discovery. When LA 1426 returned to fleet colours in November 1993, 56 different subjects had been advertised on the bodies of Glasgow's Atlanteans.

Some facts associated with Glasgow Atlantean AOAs are:-

- no vehicles below LA 211 were selected to carry an advertising livery,
- no buses between LA 501 and LA 600 were selected to be an AOA bus,
- LA 1381 and LA 1438 each received four different adverts, the most any Atlantean received,
- LA 1381 spent nine years and one month out of fleet livery, the longest time in AOA liveries by any of the

A northbound LA 230, carrying its first version of the Barclaycard advert, is seen undertaking a crew change in Victoria Road opposite Larkfield Garage. The application of part of the advert on the lower front panel has led to a non standard location for the front fleetnumber. (D.G. Wilson)

city's Atlanteans: only LA 1402 spent longer out of fleet livery by virtue of carrying City Tour/Coach livery.

- no buses above LA 1446 carried an AOA, nor did any Atlanteans allocated to the GCT or KCB fleets.

LA 211, Carrick Furniture Store started January 1973, finished March 1974. The livery is best described as a red tartan base. At Newlands Garage for a short spell in January 1973 for service 45 before transferring to Gartcraig Garage for the same route. However, prior to the contract expiring the bus was returned to Newlands.

LA 230, Barclaycard started March 1972 and finished December 1975. Initially with a blue, white and gold livery. before the livery was revised during 1974 to an orange based scheme. Like LA 231, this bus had been at Partick Garage until it went to Larkfield for a `seven year` overhaul. Whilst undergoing their overhauls, the buses received their advertising liveries and when they returned to service, the buses had been reallocated to Larkfield Garage much to the chagrin of the crews at Partick who received half cabs in their place. During its period as an AOA the bus was regularly allocated to service 44. Following its withdrawal in 1977, LA 230 was sent to the training school where it served until 1980.

LA 231, Yellow Pages, started April 1972 and finished April 1973. Using a yellow base, (well, it could hardly be any other colour), the bus operated out of Larkfield Garage on service 43. An unusual feature of this bus was that `Yellow Pages` was placed backwards below the front windscreen, this naturally meant that car drivers, viewing the advert in their mirrors, saw the advert the correct way round. The first advertising bus to revert to fleet livery, this along with LA 695 were the only buses repainted to GCT livery following the termination of advertising contracts. I don't know about Yellow Pages, but I bet Dinky must have sold a healthy amount of their model Atlantean bus in Yellow Pages livery in the Glasgow area when LA 231 was painted. I can remember pestering my mum and dad to get me the Dinky model!

LA 284, Busy Bee, started November 1973 and finished December 1977. Using a yellow and white base, the bus was initially at Parkhead Garage for the 61 before it was accidentally sent to Larkfield Garage in February 1974 for service 43. The mistake was quickly rectified, LA 300 replaced it on the 43, and LA 284 went back to the 61. In November 1975 the bus was rescheduled to service 62, also from Parkhead Garage and later the bus was sent to Possilpark Garage for service 52. It is interesting to note that the withdrawal of this bus was delayed on account of the advert.

LA 290, Sony, started November 1972 and finished February 1975 using a pink base. Initially, at Newlands Garage for service 38/A, the bus was later put on the 45 road from the same garage in November 1973. Later the bus operated on service 2, Knightswood to Rutherglen.

LA 295, Mackays Store, started December 1972 and finished April 1975. The bus used a red and white base and its first garage as an AOA was Gartcraig. After a month, LA 295 was moved to Bridgeton Garage and by December 1973, it was at Partick Garage for service 64. This route

apparently being chosen for it passing several of the sponsor's stores. Drivers at Partick were less than endearing about this bus. As an AOA , LA 295 was often scheduled to operate the longest duties on the 64 road, seven days a week. Due to the early starts and late finishes, this left little time for the mechanics to get to work on the bus and naturally this led to the bus being a donkey. In the end the drivers refused to have anything to do with the bus which caused consternation to the management. With Mackays having stores all along the 64 route, what if they noticed the bus was missing? The bus was soon fixed and put back on the road and for a few weeks it was a flyer again. However those long schedules soon caught up with the bus and it was soon back in the condition it was in prior to being blacked by the drivers. LA 295 was far from unique and drivers from several garages have all mentioned that the AOA buses were often the worst buses in their garage to drive. LA 295 also appeared on service 43, Ruchill to Cathcart, but unfortunately there are no further details.

LA 300, Krazy House, started December 1973 and finished May 1978. The bus was first painted white/yellow/White/purple in a style similar to the GGPTE livery, but it later appeared in a revised layout. Started in December 1973 at Bridgeton Garage on service 64, but in the spring of 1974 it moved to Larkfield Garage for service 43. By June LA 300 was on the move again, this time to Possilpark Garage for the 52 and in October it was put to work on service 6 from Gartcraig Garage. By April 1975, the livery had been revised and the bus reentered service on route 18/A from Possilpark and later saw use on service 54 from the same garage. October 1975 saw LA 300 at Parkhead garage for service 13 and in February 1976 it was off to Partick Garage for service 15. July saw it back at Parkhead for service 62 and in September it appeared on service 9 from Knightswood Garage. LA 300 was finally withdrawn in the spring of 1978 and like LA 284 its withdrawal was delayed on account of the advertisement.

LA 302, M&W Personnel, started June 1974 and finished March 1977 using a pink and white base. Despite having been converted for use as an omo bus, LA 302's first duties as an AOA were on Bridgeton Garage crew route 18 in June 1974. Later allocations included, Knightswood Garage in September 1975 for service 2, Partick Garage in February 1976 for service 64 and Possilpark Garage for service 45 in July 1976.

LA 381 carried an allover advert for Transcard, the Executive's travel card and started in September 1974 with a yellow and white base. This was revised to a blue base colour in July 1976 and this new version was carried until the withdrawal of LA 381 in July 1979. First port of call for LA 381 as an AOA was Possilpark Garage for service 28 in September 1974. By September 1975, the bus had moved over to Maryhill Garage and was allocated to general duties. The bus was still at Maryhill in August 1976 after its livery was revised. After withdrawal LA 381 was sold to Boyce of Glasgow who used the bus between September 1979 and February 1982. After this, the bus appears to have become an engineless seat store in the yard of Stewart of Dalmuir.

LA 391, Cameron and Campbell, a local Renault motor car dealership, commenced advertising in December 1974

LA 284 in Busy Bee disguise, above, is seen in the city centre on service 62 which operated out of Parkhead Garage. Note that despite the age of the bus, black fleetnumberplates have been fitted. (David G. Wilson)

LA 302, below, carrying its M&W Personnel advert. Note the split windscreen and additional direction indicators on the front dash when comparing this bus to LA 230 on page 86. (A.J. Douglas)

using a blue, white and yellow scheme and ran until January 1976. The bus was used initially in this guise from Gartcraig Garage for service 38/A. However by March 1975, it was at Knightswood Garage for service 2.

LA 404, Agnews Stores, a well known Glasgow off licence chain in the seventies, while using a white base started the advert in February 1975 and ran until April 1977, the bus being allocated initially to Possilpark Garage for service 54 and from September 1975 was allocated to Maryhill Garage for service 61.

LA 425 with an advert for Rank CityWall/ Savoy Suite which started in June 1975 and ran until September 1976 using purple and white as the base colours. In June 75 the bus was employed on service 66 from Larkfield Garage. However by October the bus had developed nomadic traits. Although still at Larkfield the bus was unallocated to a specific route in the morning and would take up a 44 duty in the afternoon. This changed in November when the bus was given an all day diagram on service 44.

LA 429, Greater Glasgow Health Board, started August 1975 and ran to September 1976 using a blue base. The bus was initially used from August 75 onwards by Possilpark Garage on route 52. In February 1976 LA 429 was sent to Newlands Garage for service 38/A. Barely a month later, the bus was at Larkfield Garage for services 43/4 before winding up on service 2 from the same garage in July.

LA 439, Citizen's Theatre, the advert started in August 1975 and finished September 1976 using a red, green, gold and black base. From September 75, the bus appeared on service 2 from Larkfield Garage, but the bus had another claim to fame. In November 1976 the BBC children's television programme 'Take a ticket to ' came to the city and LA 439 was used to visit different sites within the city. Venues that were visited included the Fossil Grove in Victoria Park, George Square, the Paddle Steamer Waverley and a Clydeside shipyard.

LA 442, Maryhill Carpets, started in August 1975 and ran until December 1978 on a mauve and blue base. The first of three AOAs, all of which carried a different livery, for Big Peter who ran a chain of Carpet Stores across the city during the seventies and early eighties. Initially put to work from Parkhead Garage on service 61, Tollcross to Maryhill, the bus was reallocated to Knightswood Garage in December 1976 for service 2.

LA 476, D.H.Milne, started January 1976 and ran until June 1976. A blue base was used to advertise this city photographer and during its short period as an AOA, LA 476 could be found operating on service 2 from Knightswood Garage. The advert was prematurely terminated on account of the sponsor going out of business.

LA 480, Escariot, started December 1975 and finished March 1977. The bus used a white and black base and was allocated to Maryhill Garage for service 1.

LA 489, Blazes and Berkeley, started February 1976 and ran until August 1978. The advert for these city centre establishments used a white and pink base. Initially at Knightswood Garage in February 76 for service 44, the bus was sent to Newlands Garage in September 76 for service 38/A. Barely had the bus settled in south Shawlands and it was off to Maryhill Garage in November 76 for unknown duties.

LA 636, the second AOA for Maryhill Carpets, started

When this photo of LA 404 in Glassford Street was taken in March 1977, it wasn't just Agnews that gave change but also the PTE's buses. Despite the 'Please Pay Driver' sign and Ultimate ticket machine being clearly visible in the front windscreen, ' no change' buses in the city were still just a pipedream for crews. (D. Cousins)

November 1978 when it replaced LA 442 and ran until October 1981. This time a red and white base was applied to the bus and was a regular on service 61.

LA 692, Everton Mints, started June 1973 and finished December 1974. Although delivered in GCT livery, the bus was sent to Larkfield Bus Works for repainting as an AOA prior to entering service. LA 692 was painted with black and white vertical stripes to replicate the sweets, although it also resembled a large zebra on wheels. Put to work on service 60 from Parkhead Garage, the bus had to be reallocated to service 13 from the same garage in the autumn of 74 when problems with the aqueduct in Maryhill Road led to height clearance problems that necessitated a route change for LA 692 whilst repairs were carried out.

LA 695 carried a broadside advert for Castrol GTX motor oil from July 1973 until August 1974. Using a white base painted between decks, LA 695 carried the first broadside advert on a bus in Scotland. The advert having simply been applied over its as delivered GCT livery. When the advert came to an end the bus was rather surprisingly repainted back into full GCT livery rather than GGPTE livery. Such was the rapidity of repainting LA 691– 716, that by March 1974 only LA 695 and one other Atlantean fitted with engine shrouds retained GCT livery. Anyway, the bus operated out of Newlands Garage.

LA 701, Balmore Bakery, started September 1973 and finished December 1974. With the advert applied to a white base LA 701 operated out of Bridgeton Garage on service 63. The advert had been scheduled to come off the bus during November 1974. However a strike by GGPTE staff led to the repainting of the bus being delayed by three weeks.

LA 739, PTE Recruitment, started June 1974 and finished November 1975 on a white, yellow and green base. The bus was initially used as a mobile recruitment office until October 1974. LA 739 is listed as being at Larkfield Garage in November 74, but by February 1975, the livery had been amended and the bus converted to single door before being sent to Bridgeton Garage for service 64. From November 1975 until December 1976 the bus carried a Transrail advert on behalf of the PTE. Using a white, maroon and black base LA 739 had the look of an Edinburgh Atlantean about it. The route and garage allocations remained unchanged until April 76 when it was allocated to Bridgeton's share of service 18/A. With the closure of Bridgeton in May 76, LA 739 went to Partick Garage.

LA 768, Diamond Heavy Lager, started May 1980 and finished June 1981 on a red base.

LA 775, Phoenix Assurance, started June 1980 and ran until June 1983. Using a navy blue base the bus had more than a passing resemblance to Midland Scottish buses. This must have caused some confusion in the northern parts of the city where both PTE and Midland buses operated. The bus saw use on services 6, 20 and later 54/A although, unfortunately, the garages are unknown.

LA 850, Carlsberg Lager, commenced October 1975 and finished November 1978, painted in a distinctive all over yellow on the nearside and all over red on the offside with lettering proclaiming ` Carlsberg draught keeps ahead.` Sadly it was not good enough to stop LA 850 loosing its head in June 1982 when the bus was converted to a single decker, SA 1. When still a double decker, the bus was at Partick Garage in November 1975 for service 63 and was transferred to Knightswood Garage in April 1976 for service 9. It didn't stop long here, however, as it appeared at Newlands Garage in July 76 for service 45.

LA 995, Transcard, advertised from November 1977 to November 1979 using a green base. Another bus to be given

LA 995 leads a procession of buses including an unidentified LA 751-1100 Atlantean across Glasgow Bridge. Whilst the wee boys playing up for the camera on LA 995 draw your attention, the hidden jewel in this picture is the Western SMT Bristol Loddekka bringing up the rear of the two Atlanteans. (D. Cousins)

the AOA treatment to advertise the PTE`s travel ticket, initially put to work from Ibrox Garage in November 1977 and later saw use on service 54.

LA 1062, Fastfare, commenced May 1979 and ran until January 1981 with a white base. The bus was used to introduce and promote to the Glasgow public the impending conversion to ` no change` buses by the PTE.

LA 1135, Silver Jubilee/ Bell's Whisky ran from March 1977 until June 1978. With the arrival of the Queen's Silver Jubilee the PTE had painted seven Atlanteans in all over silver with sky blue waistbands. It is interesting to note that as Lothian didn't have any facilities for spray painting, the PTE also spray painted Lothian's Silver Jubilee Atlanteans. Whilst most of the buses saw use on the city tour, LA 1135/ 42 were used on normal services. LA 1135 entered service on Good Friday 1977 at Knightswood Garage and was put to work on route 2. Later the bus appeared at Larkfield Garage and operated on the 59 during July 77, service 43 in November 77 and service 44 in January 78.

LA 1239, Bell's Whisky was displayed from May 1978 to June 1979 in a silver based livery that was a variation to the Silver Jubilee livery used on LA 1135/42, essentially the references to the Queen having been removed. Subsequently this livery became synonymous with the Bells Whisky

buses over the next decade.

LA 1240, Bell's Whisky, from May 1978 to June 1979 on a silver base was operated out of Larkfield Garage and saw use on the 77 Centre Circle service.

LA 1259, Barrowland Market, commenced March 1980 and ran until June 1983, using a cream base. The bus operated on the 62 from Parkhead Garage and later saw use on service 54, garage unknown.

LA 1266, Wellhall Garage—Lada/ Saab Dealer started April 1979 and finished August 1981 and operated on service 18/A.

LA 1293/4 both carried Bell's Whisky adverts from June 1979 to June 1981 in the now customary silver.

LA 1304 , Lloyds Brothers/Yamaha Motorcycles, started July 1979 on the delivery of the bus and ran until June 1981 using a white base. There is scant information on LA 1304, but it did operate on service 44.

LA 1315, Alan Stewart Hairdresser, started April 1983 to June 1984 on a blue base with the bus running from Knightswood Garage on service 20.

LA 1341, Blindcraft broadside advert appeared from June 1988 to July 1991. Employing a white base, LA 1341 was initially put to work from Larkfield Garage before being reallocated to Possilpark Garage which was located

The other Silver Jubilee Atlantean to be operated in normal service, LA 1142, ran from April 1977 until June 1978. For a very short period in May 1977 the bus was at Parkhead Garage for service 1 before being sent to Newlands Garage for service 45 and in July this garage put the bus to work on the 38/A road. Larkfield Garage finally got its hands on the bus in November and allocated the bus to the 77, Centre Circle service, which had been acquired from Partick Garage on its closure earlier in the year. (David.G.Wilson)

near to the Blindcraft factory.

LA 1351, Sony/ Video One , started October 1981 and finished June 1983 with a white base.

LA 1355, Victor Devine Motorcycles, commenced October 1981 and ran until November 1984 using a white base. Following the extension of service 21 to Kessington in April 1982, this bus was frequently used on this route by Newlands Garage. The author used to be fascinated by this bus which always did the 0850 departure from Kessington. Midland Scottish used Northern Counties bodied Daimler Fleetline MRF 107 on the parallel SBG service and it looked drab and boring when compared to LA 1355 which had a high driving position and plush seating. Another advantage of the bus was that if you happened to be on the third or fourth floor of Boclair Academy around 1320, you could tell by the advert that LA 1355 had returned. A quick consultation of the timetable and it could be seen that the 21 schedule ran as:- Kessington– Pollok– Renfrew Street– Pollok– Kessington.

LA 1356, Maryhill Shopping Centre was advertised from December 1981 to May 1983 using a red base. Whilst in this guise the bus appeared on service 61. After a period in fleet livery and unusual for the time, LA 1356 gained a second AOA in February 1985 for Whitehead– Dexion Storage Centre. Allocated to Parkhead Garage, the bus had a black base and operated on service 1.

LA 1381, Chisholm Hunter Jewellers, started November 1982 and finished October 1983 on a blue base. LA 1381 was at Parkhead Garage whilst advertising Chisholm Hunter Jewellers and was usually on service 62. On the advert finishing, the bus was instantly repainted with a ` Glasgow 2000– No Smoking` advert on a white base which was sponsored by Glasgow District Council. The bus spent some time operating from Larkfield but the regular haunt in this guise was service 61 from Parkhead Garage. The practice of AOAs operating from Larkfield, when not allocated there, is almost certainly associated with the buses being sent to Larkfield by their home garage for amendments to their livery or for work to be carried out on the vehicles themselves. In October 1987 advert livery number three appeared to the order of Landmark Furniture Stores and again a white base was applied with the bus staying at Parkhead for service 61. However the advert which was carried until February 1990 had fleet livery applied to the front of the bus. With the advent of deregulation in October 1986 all Strathclyde Buses AOAs were subsequently finished in this manner. February 1990 saw the livery revised for the opening of a new Landmark store in Clydebank and the bus returned to service 62 which passed through Clydebank on its way to Faifley. Finally in December 1991 LA 1381 was repainted into SBL orange and black.

LA 1408 had an advert for SAS from December 1985 to August 1988. Now the SAS in question here is – Scandinavian Air Services – not guys in black overalls who have a penchant for machine guns, hand grenades

LA 1341 pauses for breath at Govan Bus Station whilst operating the anti-clockwise part of the Inner Circle. The Inner Circle service had its origins in a Greater Glasgow Transportation Study from 1965 that proposed three circular services that would ring the city at different radii from the city centre. In the event only one of these services came to fruition. (Billy Nicol)

and visiting some of the world's most inhospitable places! Right, now that is cleared up, let's talk about the bus! LA 1408 operated on service 38/A, garage unknown, during its time as an AOA and was also allocated to Larkfield for the 59. Besides being the last Atlantean in service in Glasgow, it is at the present time the only Glasgow Atlantean to have carried an AOA that has made it into preservation. I know LA 391`s roof is on LA 320, but that doesn't count!

LA 1409, Citroen Glasgow, started July 1989 and ran until September 1991. Finished in a purple livery with an orange front, the bus was initially put to work on service 62 from Parkhead Garage. This would have led to the bus passing the Citroen dealership in Finneston, but before long the bus was operating on service 44 from Knightswood Garage. Just prior to the advert being removed the bus appeared several times on service 21 from Larkfield Garage.

LA 1411, Laing Homes broadside advert started January 1984 and ran until June 1987 on a green and yellow base. LA 1411 was unique amongst the SBL broadside adverts in that it had neither black window surrounds nor a black skirt whilst in the first version of this livery. This bus had a nomadic life in advert mode as it was frequently allocated to routes passing close to Laing developments. Started out at Newlands Garage operating on service 21 in which it took over the schedule of LA 1355 and also service 45 from the same garage. October 1987 saw the livery revised to carry the advert on a white base and the front of the bus was repainted into fleet colours with LA 1411 being put to

work from Larkfield Garage on service 59 and later from Knightswood Garage on service 16.

LA 1412, Thomson Music Stores ran from June 1985 until December 1986 on a purple base. Operated from Parkhead Garage on service 18 in this guise before the bus was repainted as an Allied Carpets AOA in December 1986. This latter advert, which had a blue base and orange front, was carried until October 1988 and the bus could be found on service 38/A from the same garage.

LA 1414, Fuji Audio Tapes, started January 1989 and finished March 1990. The bus which was painted with a white base and orange front, ran from Parkhead Garage on service 62 and complimented LA 1438 which also carried an identical Fuji Audio Tapes advert during the same period.

LA 1417 carried a Candleriggs advert on a white base. Little detail has surfaced about this bus, but it did operate on service 62A out of Knightswood Garage.

LA 1423, Archers Car Dealership, began December 1986 and finished July 1988. Painted in a red and black livery with fleet colours on the front, the bus was a regular on service 9 out of Knightswood Garage. During the period of this advert the bus hit a tenement block in Drumchapel`s Lillyburn Place. The retrieval of the bus was an intricate affair that took several hours. When LA 1423 returned to service, it was fitted with a reverse style of LA 751 destination display identical to the one on LA 1332. On return to SBL livery the bus remained at Knightswood

LA 1381 heads east on Dumbarton Road in Partick whilst carrying its fourth and final advertising livery. As a result of deregulation, Strathclyde Buses chose to retain fleet livery on the front of its buses carrying allover adverts. (Billy Nicol)

Garage and gained a rear end advert for Glasgow Brickyard on a white base. Not the luckiest of buses, LA 1423`s career was terminated by fire damage whilst operating on service 20 in East Kilbride . The fire apparently was so severe that the some of the aluminum panels began to melt and some metallic fragments were embedded in the tarmac afterwards.

LA 1425, Henry Brothers Car Dealership, started March 1986 and finished February 1988. Painted in a black and white livery, the bus operated on service 44 from Knightswood Garage.

LA 1426, BP Dome of Discovery was carried on the very last Atlantean to wear an AOA for SBL. Despite the Atlantean still being the most common chassis in the fleet, the company now used newer vehicles for future AOAs. The advert began in May 1990 and ended in November 1993. Painted in a two tone blue base with orange front, the bus was initially a regular performer from Knightswood Garage on service 9A which passed the Dome. Later LA 1426 saw use on services 44 and 51 from the same garage.

LA 1429, displayed Sport For All from April 1986 to June 1987. The advert was sponsored by The Scottish Sports Council. Initially, the bus was based at Gartcraig Garage. However after its closure LA 1429 went to Parkhead Garage and the bus was often allocated to service 41/A which ran from the city centre to Easterhouse.

LA 1430 displayed Stepek Electrical Stores on a white base. Running from September 1984 until May 1986, this was another bus to carry a broadside advert. Based at Parkhead Garage, the bus was a regular on service 62.

LA 1432, Wimpey Homes, started April 1985 and ran until May 1987 on a cream base.

LA 1435, Gold Centre, started July 1981 and finished November 1982. Using a gold base, naturally, the bus was allocated initially to Maryhill Garage for service 61 and later to Parkhead Garage for the same route.

LA 1436, Fostering Campaign, started March 1981 and finished June 1982 carrying a red based livery. Whilst the bus entered service in this livery, it is not known what livery the bus carried when it headed south for an inspection of its security screen by Yorkshire Traction the previous month.

LA 1437/8 were the next two buses to carry the silver Bell's Whisky adverts. Replacing LA 1293/4 in June 1981, the promotion ran until May 1983 on LA 1437 and July 1983 on LA 1438. That the Atlanteans were replaced by Ailsas A 79/80 as Bell's Whisky Buses in May 1983 is early proof that the Atlantean dynasty in Glasgow was now heading towards the terminus. Whilst silver, LA 1438 was at Larkfield Garage for use on service 59. Barely stopping for breath, LA 1438 appeared in July 1983 painted in a green, white and red scheme to the order of the Jolly Giant Toy Store. The advert lasted until November 1984 and the

LA 1426 is in Jamaica Street on a cross city journey from Drumchapel to South Nitshill via Partick. The recess around the numberplate was found on new examples of LA 1311 to LA 1449 Atlanteans, but became rare as the buses aged. Also noticeable on the front panel is a patch over the removed omo sign. (Billy Nicol)

bus could be found running out of Knightswood Garage on service 44 and occasional forays on service 16 which passed the Jolly Giant Store in Crow Road. Photographic evidence also places the bus at Newlands Garage on services 21 and 45 although there are no dates available. Then followed a period of two years back in fleet livery before LA 1438 appeared in its third AOA scheme, a white based livery for Klick Photopoint/ Munro Drycleaners. Running from September 1986 until August 1988, the bus once again operated out of Knightswood Garage, but this time on service 44. Another period in SBL livery then ensued before the fourth and final AOA for LA 1438 was applied in January 1989. With a white base, the advert for Fuji Audio Tapes would last until March 1990 and as previously noted,

complimented the identical advert on LA 1414. The bus continued to operate from Knightswood Garage with the chosen route this time being service 9.

LA 1441, Maryhill Carpets, started July 1982 and finished December 1983. Appearing nine months after LA 636 had returned to fleet colours, LA 1441 was the third and final AOA for Big Peter. Using a white base the bus appeared on service 38/A.

LA 1446, Parkhead Forge, started July 1985 and finished March 1987. Using a white base, numerically LA 1446 was the highest numbered Atlantean to be chosen for the AOA treatment and operated from Parkhead Garage on service 61.

LA 1441 is seen inside Larkfield Bus Works receiving attention . In the background one of the former National Bus Company Leyland Leopards acquired by SPTE is being prepared as a tow truck for the bus fleet. (David.G. Wilson)

The Other Chassis

After 1962, Glasgow virtually standardised on buying Leyland Atlanteans until the start of the eighties. Whilst Glasgow turned to Ailsas, Leyland Olympians and MCW Metrobuses, other concerns, like Greater Manchester and Merseyside, continued buying Atlanteans, along with second generation chassis, until 1984, when Leyland stopped offering the Atlantean to the U.K. market. Excluding buses that could never have been an Atlantean, the Seddon midibuses and coaches etc., what were these other chassis that were purchased by GCT and its successors? As noted earlier, between August 1962 and the formation of GGPTE in June 1973, GCT purchased 694 Atlanteans and just 17 buses on other chassis.

The first of these buses was Daimler Fleetline D 268, SGD 730. Carrying the same style of Alexander body that had been fitted to the Atlanteans, the bus was purchased in 1963 and allocated to Maryhill Garage. Mr Fitzpayne was keen to have a Fleetline in the fleet as he felt this might make Leyland more competitive when it submitted its tenders to GCT. Should Leyland fail to submit the best tender, Mr Fitzpayne felt that having operating experience of the Fleetline would be useful when it came to looking at an alternative chassis supplier. Almost externally identical to the Atlantean fleet, it was only given away when moving by its Fleetline whine as opposed to the throaty roar of an Atlantean. Mechanically, D268 came fitted with a Gardner 6LX engine, fluid flywheel and Diamatic semi automatic gearbox with electric gearchange on the steering column. This one-off purchase made sporadic appearances in the bus fleet and it was off the road for over a year in the early seventies. In 1974 D 268 was withdrawn with only 156 000 miles on the clock, which was about half the mileage a similar aged Atlantean would have run up. Prior to being withdrawn, D 268 was painted in GGPTE livery and fitted with LA 751 style fleetplates to allow it to be displayed at Larkfield Garage for the 1974 Presidential visit of the Omnibus Society. In 1975 the bus was sold to Grahams of Paisley, becoming D 15 and gave its new owner four years of service.

D 268 was almost joined by a second Fleetline later in the year. At the 1963 Kelvin Hall Show, a second Alexander bodied Fleetline, 565 CRW, appeared in GCT livery. The bus was almost finished to Glasgow specification and even had a GCT embossed saloon mirror fitted. Incredibly, the mirror was still on the bus in 1975. In the aftermath of a Kelvin Hall Show, the Corporation would usually purchase exhibits that had been displayed in their livery. Mr Fitzpayne was keen to purchase the bus and it was for sale at £ 7 047, ex works. The Corporation were not so keen to purchase the bus and it became a demonstrator until Grahams of Paisley purchased it in 1967.

The other 16 chassis purchased by GCT between August 1962 and June 1973 were 16 Leyland Panthers. The first Panther, 36 foot long LS 31, arrived in 1964 and carried a dual door Alexander `W` type body, which seated 42 passengers and allowed 31 standees. By the time the bus entered service in 1965, the need for saloons in the fleet had been diminished by the lowering of the roadway under the railway line in Hillington Road. From the middle of May 1964, double deck buses had been able to enter Hillington Estate from the south. This led to double deck service 15 being extended into the estate and gave the first direct connection to the city centre via this route. Two services, 24 and 30, still needed saloons. However, due to height problems, the Panthers were unsuitable and thus they were to be found on service 21 which could accommodate Atlanteans as it had no height restrictions.

LS 32 followed during 1965 and appeared at the 1965 Kelvin Hall Show before entering service on service 21 in February 1966. LS 33, when ordered had been originally an Atlantean and made its debut at the 1967 Kelvin Hall Show. Ironic really, as outside the show LA 362 was extolling the benefits of one man double deck operation. By the time the rest of this one time Atlantean order arrived, LS 34– 46, the go ahead had been given for double deck omo in Glasgow.

During 1970, services 24 and 30 were rerouted allowing the Panthers to replace the last Leyland Worldmasters on these routes. Incredibly, Panther withdrawals started in May 1971 with LS 31/2 and the following month, LS 33. Along with later withdrawn LS 38, all three buses would be handed over to GGPTE in June 1973, but would not see service again. The Panthers were on shaky ground however, Atlanteans temporarily replacing them on service 24, Gairbraid Avenue to Cadder, from late 1973 to March 1974. The fleet was now in steady decline and LS 40 was withdrawn during 1974 with further withdrawals seeing the end of LS 34/6/7/9 in 1975 and LS 42– 5 in 1977. Overhaul work during 1976 saw Atlanteans substituting for Panthers on service 30, Sandyhills– North Carntyne, which was operated by Gartcraig Garage. The route was split into two sections, Sandyhills to Vesalius Street and Cockenzie Street to North Carntyne, with through booking available. In 1977 service 30 was rerouted to operate between North Carntyne and Sandyhills via Shettleston. The diversion took the route away from a low bridge in Carntyne and effectively spelt the end for the Panthers. A shortage of Atlanteans at Gartcraig Garage earned the buses a temporary reprieve and the Panthers could be found operating services 6/41/2 during the peaks. Subsequently LS 35/43/6 were rebuilt as coaches and became C2 –4, the vehicles finding use on private hires as well as the city tour before they were sold off in 1981.

By the mid seventies, having purchased both Daimler and Bristol, Leyland had become the dominant chassis supplier in the British market. It intended to replace both the Atlantean and the Fleetline with a new product, initially known as the B15 and later changed to the Titan - a curious choice of name as the PD3 Titan had only ceased production towards the end of the sixties and large numbers of youthful half cab PD 3 Titans remained on Britain's roads. The latest Titan, however, bore no relation to its half cab predecessor, having a fully automatic gearbox, full air suspension, better internal headroom and quieter engine noise. Unlike an Atlantean, the new Titan's steering wheel was only 18 inches across. Controversially, the bus had an integral chassis and Park Royal was to be the supplier of the bodywork. For provincial operators who had nurtured good relationships with their local bodybuilder this was most unpopular.

Prototype NHG 732P visited Glasgow in December 1975 and was used only for staff transport. Mr Cox was a fan of Leyland's new baby and definitely wanted the bus for Glasgow. In the summer of 1977 the PTE announced that five Titans had been ordered with delivery to start in December 1978. The PTE planned to evaluate the Titan against the other new kid on the block, the MCW Metrobus, to help decide future orders. In the end no Titans were delivered to Glasgow, with the order being quietly dropped in 1979, Atlantean orders were to continue for a few more years while Leyland revised thc Titan concept.

A Titan did however appear in Glasgow wearing GGPTE livery. Prototype 02 was displayed at the 1977 Kelvin Hall Show in single door form wearing PTE livery. Prior to appearing in Glasgow, the bus had undergone overhaul and modifications, including the removal of the centre door.

Out of the Titan came the Leyland Olympian, which unlike the Titan offered operators the chance to select their preferred bodybuilder. The first Olympian for the PTE, LO 1, was the third Olympian prototype and had chassis code B45 rather than chassis code ON as the remainder of the PTE's Olympians delivered until 1984 would get. With air suspension, Hydracyclic gearbox and Leyland's TL 11 engine, this was no rehashed Atlantean. LO 1 made its public appearance at the Birmingham Motor Show in November 1980 in the National Exhibition Centre. Carrying the prototype Alexander `R` type bodywork, LO 1 wore the third stage PTE livery of yellow/black/green with `Strathclyde` fleetnames. Such was Alexanders' faith in this new body that it gave a 15 year guarantee on each `R` type body. Unusually for the time, LO 1 had a Luminator electronic destination display fitted which flashed intermediate points as well as ultimate destinations at intending passengers. The Luminator screen in time would be changed for conventional roller blinds, however, with the passage of time, electronic destination displays have become commonplace in Britain's bus industry. After the show, the bus went on demonstration duties before entering service at Maryhill Garage in June 1981, by which time the fleetnames had been changed to `Trans-Clyde`. It is interesting to record that during 1981 LO 1 wasn't the only B45 Olympian in north west Glasgow. The Scottish Bus Group evaluated an ECW bodied B45 Olympian at Midland's Milngavie Garage for a while. Unfortunately LO 1, was destroyed in the Larkfield Fire in May 1992.

Over the following two and a half years, another 45 Olympians would join the fleet. LO 2– 11 came at the end of 1981 with highbridge bodies by Charles Roe of Leeds, the first buses for Glasgow from this company. ECW lowheight bodies were specified on LO 12– 16 which were delivered in early 1982. All of the ECW Olympians delivered up to LO 46 carried the lowheight 13 feet 8 inch body. In the post deregulation years, these buses would be needed to reach East Kilbride via the restricted height clearance Busby railway bridge. LO 17– 21 saw a return to Alexanders bodywork and also saw the first Olympians with the large Ailsa type destination screens. Unlike SBG Olympians,

LS 31 wearing the reverse livery that single deck omo buses wore, poses for the camera. Note that the windows between the entrance and exit are taller than the windows to the rear of the exit. (D.G.Wilson Collection)

the PTE`s buses were full height and had a half window aft of the offside stairwell. Spring 1983 saw a return to ECW bodywork with LO 22– 41 being the last Olympians delivered in the third stage PTE livery. LO 42– 46 were delivered in December 1983 in the fourth stage PTE livery.

Following trials with Leyland Nationals on service 97, Shawlands– Hillpark and Mansewood, an order for Atlanteans was curtailed by twenty chassis and replaced by a like number of Nationals which arrived in the spring of 1979. The buses were delivered, unusually for the city, with moquette seating and wore an all white livery, although prior to entering service most of the buses were given a yellow and green skirt. The Nationals, like the Panthers a decade earlier, were virtually surplus to requirements before they arrived. LN 17/9/20 were sent to Islay in May 1979, still all over white, to replace the services of Maroner Coaches before seeing any city service. LN 17/20 finally entered service in Glasgow during October 1979, by which time LN 17 wore the coach livery of white and ochre. LN 19, on the other hand, would not see use in the city until June 1980! Following the cessation of Garelochead Motor Services, whose varied fleet included some Atlanteans, Parkhead based LN 6/8/13/18– 20 were all loaned to Phibbs of Helensburgh for a few weeks in September 1980. Phibbs had partially replaced part of Garelochead`s network, but didn't have any certified omo buses to carry out the work. Some Nationals did find use in the city, service 97, and the inter station service 98 providing limited employment for some. Others found themselves on short term loans to operators like Mc Nairs of Girvan, LN 2/13, and Millport Motors, LN 14. Although the Nationals did get repainted into the orange and black livery of Strathclyde Transport, they were really surplus to use and by the time of deregulation, most were languishing in the reserve fleet. A few Nationals, LN 1 included, managed to soldier on until the end of National operations in May 1987 and LN 20 was subsequently retained for use as a publicity vehicle. After their withdrawal most of the Nationals ended up in England, although LN 14/5 went to Millport Motors and LN 16 appeared with Mc Gills of Barrhead. The good news for National fans is that LN 1 has been secured for preservation and currently resides within the Transport Preservation Trust in Beith.

1972 marked a sea change in both Glasgow's relationship with Leyland and also its blind loyalty to the Atlantean. To provide a comparison with the Atlantean, 20 MCW Metropolitans, M1– 20 were ordered. They would be delivered in 1974, by which time GGPTE was responsible for the bus fleet and were closely followed by a further 20 buses, M 21– 40. The bus combined Scania mechanical units with an MCW body and came with automatic transmission and an 11 litre engine. These big, impressive machines, which only carried PTE 1 livery, could show a clean pair of heels when required, but unfortunately they tended to slide in wintry conditions and were notoriously heavy on fuel. Despite these problems the thing that finished off the Metropolitan was corrosion of the metal body frame, a problem that continued with both MCW`s Metrobus and Metrorider offerings. Withdrawals started in 1979 and by the summer of 1982 they were all gone, just before the final

few needed new certificates of fitness, or costly overhaul and repair to you and me.

Just as the Titan spawned the Olympian, so the Metropolitan mutated into the MCW Metrobus. Now wholly built in the U.K., the new chassis came with air suspension, Voith gearbox and a Gardner 6LXB engine. Prototype TOJ 592S visited Glasgow in April 1978 and operated on service 2, Knightswood to Rutherglen. Despite having a separate entrance and exit, the prototype operated with just the front doors operational, the PTE`s dalliance with dual doors was definitely over.

With similarities to the Metropolitan, it was no surprise that the PTE initially allocated fleetnumbers in the M series. On the 17th April 1979, Alexander (Midland) and the PTE both received their first Metrobuses in a handing over ceremony at Buchannan Bus Station in Glasgow. The Midland example MRM 1 would carry an Alexander body, and a rare one at that, the PTE example was bodied by MCW and wore fleetnumber MB 3 externally, internally it wore fleetnumber M 43. Initially the batch was put to work from Parkhead Garage in July 1979, but later the buses moved to Maryhill Garage when it became the evaluation garage.

MB 6– 20 arrived in May 1982 and carried highbridge Alexander `R` type bodies, the Ailsa style destination display debuting on Metrobuses with this batch. Spring 1983 saw MCW bodies back in vogue with the arrival of MB 21– 35, which carried the Mark 2 body with its revised front dash and windscreen arrangement.

MB 22 was reseated with coach seats in May 1984 and repainted in coach livery. MB 23-6 followed soon after, although not finished to such high standards as MB 22. MB 36– 45 arrived in the autumn of 1983 and were the first Metrobuses to be delivered in the orange and black livery. Whilst MB 21– 43 had Garner 6LXB engines fitted, the final two buses, MB44/5, had Cummins L 10 power units. Although all 45 Metrobues had Voith gearboxes, two different units were employed, the three speed D 851 and the four speed D 854. When Maryhill Garage closed in 1984 the Metrobuses moved to Possilpark Garage, and were joined by a further 25 examples that were delivered in 1989.

GGPTE had operated Ailsa Volvo demonstrator THS 273M in September 1974. The bus operated from Larkfield Garage on the Castlemilk routes in Alexander (Midland) blue with a SBG triangle screen and short bay bodywork. Alan Westwell could see a future for these buses that were really back to the future. With a front entrance they appeared the same to the public as an Atlantean, however unlike the Atlantean the engine was also at the front of the bus. Mr Westwell felt that the Ailsa chassis was more robust than the Atlantean and the Ailsa overcame several key problems that afflicted the Atlanteans. Ailsa were keen to build a batch of 10 pre– production models and Alan Westwell hoped that all ten would come to Glasgow with Alexanders short bay bodywork. Ronald Cox, who preferred the Alexander wide bay bodywork, was more interested in the aesthetics of a body style than its engineered strengths and weaknesses, thus the PTE only received three buses.

In the spring of 1975 the first Ailsa Volvo B55 entered

The closure of Bridgeton Garage in May 1976 meant that by March 1977, only Possilpark Garage was running MCW Metroplitans on service 18. M22 loads in Argyle Street heading for Springburn via its home garage. (Dave Cousins)

A 118, one of a pair of Ailsas to carry Marshall bodywork, is seen crossing Argyle Street in April 1997 with one of the Leyland Olympians bought in the aftermath of the Larkfield fire, LO 52, following behind. (Brian. Ridgway)

AV 12 was one of a batch of fifteen production Ailsas delivered to the PTE . Seen in the Saltmarket, these buses were instantly recognisable by their rounded roof domes from the three pre-production models, AV 1-3. (D. Cousins)

A10 carried Alexander's 'R' type bodywork and is seen leaving the 21 terminus at Kessington for Pollok. Note the narrow destination display and outward opening cab on A10. As further deliveries arrived, the Ailsas got sliding cab doors and larger destination displays. (Author)

service and although this fleet never grew above 18 buses, AV 1-18, all carried Alexander panoramic bodies. With its front mounted engine the driver gained access to the cab by the offside, a kind of front entrance half cab. Despite the limited number of vehicles in the fleet they clearly made a favourable impression on Alan Westwell. When asked by the author why he favoured the Ailsa, he replied that, ` the Ailsa chassis design was of a greater stiffness than the Atlantean and the drive line was much simpler`. Both of these factors he felt were important reasons why the Ailsa performed better than the Atlantean. After Alan Westwell departed to take control of the Tayside fleet in 1975 GGPTE didn't purchase any more Ailsas. However up in Dundee they were just beginning and over the next couple of years around 150 Ailsas were purchased by Tayside. It is interesting to speculate now, but had this self confessed supporter of the Ailsa stayed at GGPTE, would there have been as many Atlantean purchases in the 1976– 79 period? Go figure!

In typical Glasgow fashion, that there were only 18 Ailsas in the fleet didn't mean an identical fleet. AV 1-3 were part of a pre-production batch of 10 buses and were easily distinguished from AV 4– 18, their Alexander bodies having peaked front and rear domes, whilst AV 4– 18 had similar bodies to the `AL` Atlanteans in the fleet. All 18 buses gave sterling service, working only from Larkfield Garage, until the fire in May 1992 ripped this small fleet apart, nine examples being destroyed in the blaze that night. One Ailsa, AV 10, was converted to single deck following accident damage and continued in service with SBL until the mid nineties when it was sold to Black Prince of Morley. Its new owners discovered that the bus had never been given a tilt test by SBL when it was reconfigured to single deck and technically was still a double decker. Its new owners not wishing to undertake costly repairs, dispatched the bus to the scrapyard.

Mr Westwell returned to the PTE in November 1979 to become the Director General and this saw a return to favour for the Ailsa in Glasgow. It must be remembered that the Atlantean although nearing the end of its production run at Leyland, would continue being delivered to UK operators until late 1984. So it wasn't need that forced this change of chassis supplier. In June 1981 the first Mark 3 Ailsa was delivered, bodied with the Alexander `R ` type body of which all bar two of the 133 examples would wear. A1– 10 were put to work from Maryhill Garage as part of the next generation evaluation fleet. Ailsas were also delivered new to several other garages, Knightswood and Larkfield, and Possilpark operated A1– 10 for a while after Maryhill closed in May 1984. Just prior to deregulation,all the Ailsas were placed at one garage, Larkfield. Sadly, A1 was yet another first bus destroyed in the Larkfield Fire. For a while it appeared that A 10 had been bought for preservation by a group based in the West Midlands, but by 2004 it had been scrapped. When A 10 was new in 1981 it spent three months with WMPTE who repainted the bus in fleet livery during its stay in the Midlands. A 117/8 were purchased in May 1984, the only two Ailsas for the PTE not to be bodied by Alexander. Carrying Marshall bodywork the buses had been built for Volvo in 1983 and required modifications by

the PTE before they could enter service. These included the fitting of standard destination displays and repainting into SPTE livery.

In May 1982 a most unusual vehicle 31 feet 9 inches long, 14 feet 7 inches high and seating 86 passengers arrived in the fleet. With the less than aesthetic Marshall bodywork and an Ailsa badge on the front grille, what was this bus? Well, it certainly wasn't an Ailsa B55, the engine was underfloor for a start. The bus carried fleetnumber AH 1, which stood for Ailsa Horizontal, and was an amalgam of the Ailsa and Volvo B10M chassis. In simple terms AH 1 was the prototype Volvo Citybus and prior to the chassis going into production Volvo was keen to iron out any problems associated with the chassis. In common with the other new chassis at that time, AH 1 was sent to Maryhill Garage and was regularly allocated to service 61, Summerston – Tollcross. So why was such an unusual bus undergoing `in service trials` with Strathclyde PTE? The proximity of Glasgow to the Volvo plant at Irvine? Possibly, but it is more likely that AH 1 saw service in Glasgow because of input in its design and concept by Alan Westwell.

In 1984 a further five production, and revolutionary, Citybuses joined the fleet. Despite the chassis now being officially made by Volvo the new recruits, carrying non sequential numberplates A 600/1/3/2/4 TNS, were given fleetnumbers AH 2-6 instead of VC 1– 5. Bar the Citybus not having an offside driver's cab door, these buses to the casual observer could have been mistaken for Alexander bodied Ailsas such were the similarities of the two bodies. These buses were to replace the Atlanteans on the `Chauffeur Care` network and the fact that only the rear axle intruded into the lower saloon floor space meant that various combinations of layout could be accommodated in the lower saloon, as well as a larger seating capacity. AH 2– 6 entered service in April and May of 1984, although AH 4 had been displayed at the Kelvin Hall Show in November 1983. To allow wheelchair access the buses had Ratcliff hydraulic lifts fitted within the front entrance. This meant that compared to the Atlantean buses in the `Chauffeur Care` fleet, AH 2-6 had double the wheelchair capacity and more importantly a common entrance for all passengers. Internally, longitudinal tip up seating for 12 passengers allowed six wheelchairs to be accommodated in the front part of the lower saloon. Little did we know it at the time, but within 20 years fully accessible vehicles for all passengers would be the norm, not the exception. It is interesting to note that when Strathclyde Buses was in it's infancy following deregulation, Mr Westwell advised the company to purchase more Citybuses and by 1990 there were 101 such vehicles in service with SBL. Sadly AH 1 and AH 4 are yet more important Glasgow buses to have been scrapped, but AH 2/3/5/6 were still in service with First Glasgow in early 2005. With the bus preservation movement starting to get itself organised in Scotland then perhaps some of the current Glasgow buses will be saved for future generations to ponder. When one sees the wonderful efforts of the Selnec Society in Greater Manchester and the number of buses from the last 30 to 40 years in their stock, it really ought to make our official Transport Museums in Scotland blush. Is it right that Glasgow's Transport museum has three buses in it and the youngest is so old, that the author can't remember having seen it in active service?

Another one off purchase was AS 1, the unique 11 metre Ailsa B 55– 10 Mark 3 saloon. Purchased in 1983 from Volvo stock, the bus carried Marshall bodywork and was delivered wearing the blue and white livery of Tayside. Prior to entering service in April 1983 the bus was repainted into Strathclyde Transport orange and black and although a regular performer out of Larkfield Garage, the bus spent two months with Mc Nair of Girvan at the end of 1983. In later life the bus had its destination display rebuilt into a split arrangement and also acquired an Atlantean windscreen before becoming yet another victim of the Larkfield Fire.

By the autumn of 2004 AH 4 had become 31209 in the First Glasgow fleet when she caught fire on the X7 service. Apparently she was towed direct to Dunmore's from the scene of the fire. The majority of the damage was internal and although more severely damaged buses have been repaired, the age of AH 4 no doubt played a part in its demise. (Author)

The Larkfield Fire

By March 1992, six years after deregulation, the Atlantean was still the backbone of the fleet with 348 LA s in a fleet of 813 buses. The youngest, LA 1448, was over ten years old and the eldest, LA 664, besides being the last GCT bus in the service fleet, was 19 years old. New buses were thin on the ground, since deregulation the only new big buses were 95 Volvo Citybuses and 25 MCW Metrobuses that had arrived in 1988/9 and Olympians LO 47– 9 which came in 1991. In GCT or PTE days 123 buses could have arrived in little over a year. With no further new buses ordered it was apparent that Glasgow's Atlanteans still had many years ahead of them. If proof of this was needed one only had to look at the key cross city routes which were still well populated with Atlanteans.

In the early hours of the 18th May 1992 a fire broke out inside a shed at Larkfield Garage that destroyed 11 Atlanteans and 49 other buses. Some of the buses destroyed that night were of special interest. A 1 besides being the fleet's first Mark 3 Ailsa had been exhibited at the UITP conference in Dublin when new. A 40 had been an exhibit at the 1981 Kelvin Hall Show and AS 1 was the unique Volvo B55 saloon. AV 3 was one of three pre– production Ailsa Volvo B55 in the fleet that had been new in 1975. Two of the destroyed buses had been sent to Larkfield for repaints, Parkhead based AH 41 and LA 1327 from Knightswood. LO 1 was an early Olympian that carried the first Alexander R type body. LO 47 was just nine months old when destroyed. LA 1111 was the unique Atlantean to be fitted with an Ailsa style destination display. C5 had been the PTE`s first Duple bodied Leyland Leopard and C15 was the only Plaxton bodied Volvo B 10M coach in the fleet. M 113 was the last bus seated Metrorider delivered new to Strathclyde Buses. Also damaged in the fire were Volvo Ailsa A 44, the prototype Volvo Citybus AH 1 and

LA 1430, above, photographed in North Hanover Street before its destruction in the Larkfield fire. A non standard destination aperture was fitted to this bus early in its career with the PTE. Unlike the LA 1311– 50 batch, this bus has no moulding around the destination screen and although the central position for the destination screen was retained when other buses in the LA 1351– 1449 batch were modified, they retained their original large glass aperture. (B. Nicol)

MCW Metrorider M 72. By July all three of these buses were repaired and back in service. The fire was to prove the catalyst for an explosion of mid-life and elderly Atlanteans arriving in the fleet, in one night SBL had seen around 7% of its fleet go up in flames. That the buses lost in the fire would be replaced wasn't really much help on the morning after the fire. Timetables had to be maintained and although passengers would be sympathetic in the short term, that sympathy wouldn't stop them defecting to a rival operator if the SBL service became unreliable. Knowing that long term replacement buses weren't going to appear overnight, SBL initially borrowed surplus buses and, in some cases, bought buses from other operators. Those buses on loan were all given their own fleetnumber series, C 9XX, the C standing for `Contract Hire` or unofficially `Charlie`.

From Tayside came 18 dual door Ailsa Volvos which were put to work from Larkfield Garage with large signs on both sides of the centre door proclaiming ` This is not a door - no entrance`. It looked a bit daft, but it got the message across to the passengers. By the end of May Atlanteans C 924-8, from the GRT group, were in service from Knightswood Garage. Although C 924 carried Midland Bluebird livery, all had been new to Grampian Regional Transport in the 1976/7 period. Despite having Alexander bodies these were not your bog standard Glasgow `AL` bodies; these Atlanteans had peaked domes at the front and rear, like AV 1– 3, and had short bay dual door bodywork. As with the above mentioned Ailsas, SBL put them to work with the centre doors out of use. The buses were mainly used on services 9/11/16 and 20, although unidentified Grampian examples were twice seen passing through Canniesburn Toll on service 51, Linnvale—Easterhouse.

Early June saw more Atlanteans in the shape of C 918– 23 arrive on hire fromWestern Scottish. To the local enthusiast these were of interest as Western had only recently acquired the Atlanteans from Greater Manchester Buses. Not only that, C 918/9/21/2 carried Park Royal bodywork with the others carrying Northern Counties bodywork, neither of which were particularly common in the West of Scotland, let alone Glasgow. One bus, C 922, arrived still wearing GM buses livery and prior to entering service the bus was given a full repaint into SBL livery; C 918/23 would also receive full SBL livery, but in both cases these buses were repainted from Western Scottish livery. The rest of the batch were to operate with SBL fronts and rears with Western Scottish livery on their sides. It had taken 26 years, but once again Western Scottish and GCT`s successor were sharing a Park Royal bodied Atlantean. Not only that, some of the Park Royal Atlanteans were used on the 61 route, just as KTD 551C had been back in January 1966. Whilst with SBL C 920 suffered damage to its lower front panel, when it returned to service it was carrying a

C 928 is seen in Partick Bus Station . Unlike the resident Atlanteans which had 3 track number blinds, the Grampian examples were fitted with a single blind onto which the service number was printed. (Billy. Nicol)

replacement panel from GM Buses 7861, an Atlantean, complete with GM Buses livery and `QS` depot code. Thus C 920 was the only `on loan` bus to carry the liveries of three different operators simultaneously. Initially the Northern Counties bodied buses went to Knightswood Garage with the Park Royal bodied examples sent to Parkhead Garage. During their stay in Glasgow some of the Western buses would be transferred between these two garages, a unique occurrence as all the other hired in stock served at only one garage during their stint with SBL. When C 922 returned to Western in September for MOT work, this allowed a seventh ex Manchester Atlantean, C 947, to arrive from Western as its replacement. Working from Parkhead Garage the bus was put to work with only its front in SBL livery, another unique occurrence amongst hired in Atlanteans.

The final hired in Atlanteans were C 930-9 which entered service on the 2nd and 3rd of June 1992 from Larkfield Garage. Initially the buses were found on services 21, Kessington– Pollok via Merrylee and 45 Kennishead– Auchinairn. Subsequently the buses would appear on routes 12/A Barmulloch– Toryglen and 44/ A Knightswood– Newton Mearns. Such was the haste to get these buses on the road that some of them hit the streets still carrying Newcastle adverts. Besides having their front and rears in SBL livery, the ex Busways stock also carried SBL livery around the lower deck panels and windows. During August SBL bought these buses and they were allocated fleetnumbers LA 1457– 66.

C 929 was a Scania double decker that had come from Nottingham, where it was numbered 360. The bus was repainted into full SBL livery and used on a wide variety of routes. Two other Scanias, C 940/1, were Plaxton bodied saloons that could usually be found on the long 66, Mountblow– East Kilbride, route. These two buses were later bought and subsequently became SS1/2 in the fleet. The remainder of the hire buses were Daf saloons C 942 – 6, which arrived during July 1992, carrying bodywork by Ikarus, the Hungarian company.

With further Atlanteans arriving from Busways, LA 1467– 83, during the remainder of 1992, it meant that a start could be made on repatriating some of the hired in stock. December 1992 saw the withdrawal of C 901/3/ 11/5– 7/29 with C 924-8/47 returning the following month. February 1993 saw C 906/9 depart Glasgow and by June C 919/20 had returned to Western, although it would be September before all the Western Atlanteans had gone home.

In the aftermath of the fire, Strathclyde Buses placed an order for 52 Alexander bodied Leyland Olympians. These buses, which began arriving during July 1993, were amongst the last Leyland Olympians to be built by Leyland before the chassis was transferred to the Volvo plant at Irvine.

C 919 was also on loan from Western Scottish and carried the more familiar SBL livery on its front and rear only. The location is outside Kelvingrove Art Galleries where Argyle Street and Sauchiehall Street diverge. (Billy Nicol)

Listed below is a table detailing all the buses destroyed in the Larkfield Fire.

Ailsa B55– 10 Alexander H44/35F	**Leyland Olympian ON2R 50G 13Z4 Leyland H 47/31F**
AV 3 GGG 302N	LO 47 J 136FYS
AV 5/6/11– 5/7 MGE 180/1/6-90/2P	**Leyland Atlantean AN68A/1R Alexander H 45/31F**
	LA 1100 RUS 351R
Volvo Ailsa B55– 10 Alexander H 44/35F	LA 1111/4/5 TGE 830/3/5R
A 1/4 TGG 377/80W	LA 1128 TGG 743R
A 19/24/36/40 CSU 227/32/44/8X	
A 53/4/7/61 KGG 113/4/7/25Y	**Leyland Atlantean AN68A/1R Alexander H 45/33F**
A 82/4/91/6 OGG 178/80/7/92Y	LA 1306 FSU 125T
A 97/8/102 A 560/1/5SGA	LA 1327 LSU 384V
A 112 A 738PSU	LA 1407/21 RDS 596/610W
A 121/131 B 22/32YYS	LA 1430 SUS 596W
Volvo Ailsa B55– 10 Marshall	**MCW Metrorider MF 150/55 MCW B 23F**
AS 1 NHS 782Y	M 42/51/61 E 927/36/46XYS
Volvo Citybus B10M– 50 Alexander H 47/37F	**MCW Metrorider MF 154/12 MCW B33F**
AH 41 G 289OGE	M 101/13 E 198/210BNS
Leyland Olympian B 45-TL11/1R Alexander H 43/30F	**Leyland Leopard PSU 3E/4R Duple C 45FL**
LO 1 VGB 364W	C 5 BNS 234S
Leyland Olympian ONTL11/1R Roe H 44/31F	**MCW Metroliner CR 126/3/MCW C 49F**
LO 3– 5/7/11 CGG 826– 8/30/4X	C 13 A 740RNS
Leyland Olympian ONTL11/1R Alexander H 47/29F	**Volvo B10M– 55 Plaxton C 53F**
LO 20 ESU 7X	C 15 B 730CHS
Leyland Olympian ONTL11/1R ECW H47/31F	
LO 24/8 KGG 144/8Y	

Below is a complete list of the vehicles hired in by Strathclyde Buses in the aftermath of the Larkfield Fire.

C 900– 916 Volvo Ailsa B 55-10 Alexander H 44/31D Ex Tayside – Arrived 22/5/92

C 900 NSP 340R	C 904 SSN 238S	C 908 SSN 242S	C 912 SSN 251S	C 916 WTS 262T
C 901 NSP 341R	C 905 SSN 239S	C 909 SSN 243S	C 913 SSN 252S	C 917 SSN 246S
C 902 SSN 236S	C 906 SSN 240S	C 910 SSN 244S	C 914 WTS 258T	
C 903 SSN 237S	C 907 SSN 241S	C 911 SSN 248S	C 915 WTS 259T	

C 918– 923 Leyland Atlantean AN68A/1R Park Royal (918/9/21/2) or Northern Counties(920/3) Ex Western Scottish – Arrived 25/5/92

C 918 UNA 772S	C 920 ANA 211T	C 922 UNA 863S
C 919 WVM 887S	C 921 UNA 853S	C 923 RJA 702R

C 924– 928 Ley. Atlantean AN68A/1R Alex`r H 45/29D Ex Midland Bluebird (924) or Grampian (925-8) – Arrived 21/5/92 onwards

C 924 ORS 203R	C926 ORS 209R	C 928 KSA 195P
C 925 ORS 206R	C 927 KSA 192P	

C 929 Scania N 113DRB Alexander H 47/33F Ex Nottingham – Arrived May 1992

C 929 G 879TVS

C 930/1 Leyland Atlantean AN68A/1R Alexander H 45/31F Ex Busways – Arrived June 1992

C 930 JVK 234P   C 931 JVK 238P

C 932-939 Leyland Atlantean AN68A/2R Alexander H 48/31F Ex Busways – Arrived June 1992

C 932 MVK 567R	C 935 MVK 552R	C 938 MVK 512R
C 933 MVK 528R	C 936 MVK 506R	C 939 MVK 516R
C 934 MVK 502R	C 937 MVK 508R	

C 940/1 Scania N 113CRB Plaxton Verde B 51F (940) or B 47F (941) Ex Demonstrators – Arrived June 1992

C 940 J 113XSX   C 941 H 912HRO

C 942– 946 Daf SB 220 Ikarus B 48F Ex Hughes (Dealer), Daf, Cleckheaton – Arrived 10 July 1992

C 942 J 51GCX	C 944 J 53GCX	C 946 J 56GCX
C 943 J 52GCX	C 945 J 54GCX	

C 947 Leyland Atlantean AN68A/1R Park Royal H 43/32F Ex Western Scottish – Arrived September 1992

C 947 BNC 936T

In addition, two MCW Metroriders, M 123/4 (F 672/3 YOK), that had been on loan from West Midlands Travel, had their loan period extended. The buses had worn SBL livery whilst in Glasgow, but by the time of the fire, they had been repainted into West Midlands livery during May 1992 pending their return to England. In the aftermath of the fire they had their loan period extended.

On the previous page LA 1111 is seen towards the top end of Hope Street after the fitting of its non standard destination display. Service 21 was one of several PTE services to be extended beyond the city boundary in April 1982 when the rules prohibiting the majority of Scottish Bus Group buses from carrying passengers wholly within the city boundary were all but abandoned. (Billy Nicol).

GCT

In the spring of 1993, Strathclyde Buses announced that it was setting up a new subsidiary. The new company was to be known as GCT and unlike previous incarnations of these letters, this time there were no abbreviations - nothing! zilch! GCT stood only for GCT. The new company was erroneously referred to by many as a Low Cost Unit although Strathclyde Buses was having none of it. The company stated that the reason for the formation of GCT, besides helping SBL to gain more tendered bus contracts through lower costs, was to be the proving ground for new recruits to S.B. Holdings. Drivers who proved they could meet the required standards would be able to gain promotion from GCT to SBL. The company also stated that as the share capital of S.B. Holdings was 80% owned by employee shareholders, it was believed that this system would best look after the employees` interests.

Operating in a yellow and dark green livery that was separated by a black band, the new company had the official and convoluted title of Comlaw 313 Ltd. Fortunately the company traded under the GCT banner and had its registered head office at 1875 Great Western Road, Glasgow or Knightswood Garage as it is known to the man in the street. Indeed initially the company had all its buses based at Knightswood, with the shed that borders Anniesland Road and Craigend Street devoted to GCT. When operations commenced on the 1st of August 1993, GCT had an operating licence for 85 buses and it is interesting to note that although the majority of the starting fleet came from SBL, the operating licence for SBL did not drop by 85 vehicles. Thus right from the start it was plain to one and all that GCT was to be an aid to SBL in gaining extra work at lower costs and also in combating other operators. Although part of S.B. Holdings, GCT was a stand alone unit with its own wage structure and lower overheads when compared to its parent. Adverts placed in the press at the time offering work to drivers made mention of the jobs

East Lancs bodied Atlantean GLA 6, with an Alexander `AL` type front dome fitted, takes a layover in Renfield Street. In the background, the former site of the Apollo concert hall undergoes redevelopment. (B Ridgway)

being part- time with the opportunity of overtime.

When formed GCT had 50 buses and Atlanteans were the backbone of the fleet. The composition of the initial fleet was 37 Leyland Atlantean AN 68s GLA 1-37, 7 MCW Metroriders GM 1-7 and 6 Leyland Olympians GLO 1-6. The new company took over all of SBL`s night routes except for service 809, Glasgow to Bishopton. Daytime routes covered a mix of PTE supported routes, school contracts and also two interesting routes. One route was service 19, Castlemilk to Easterhouse via the City Centre. This service which had previously been operated by Kelvin Central Buses as routes 19 and 20 had been acquired by KCB from Stagecoach, who had introduced the routes as competition against SBL at the advent of de-regulation in 1986. The other route being the 100, City and SECC, which had parallels to the 77/88 Centre Circle which had operated 20 years previously, especially considering the age profile of the vehicles that GCT was using!

Prior to the commencement of operations, LA 765/1450/3– 6/67/8/71/3/5/81 were repainted from SBL to GCT livery during July 1993. As the vehicles still belonged to, and were used by, SBL until August 1st, the buses gained orange bands below the windscreens with `Strathclyde's Buses` emblazoned on them. To cover a shortage whilst these buses were being repainted, SBL returned to Tayside and hired eight Ailsas to cover the temporary shortage. It is interesting to note the similarity of the shade of dark green

used by GCT and the shade of green used by SPTE on livery experiment bus LA 947 in the early eighties. Indeed one of East Lancs bodied Atlanteans transferred to GCT wore a lighter shade of yellow than the colour that was applied to the rest of the fleet. Although services commenced at the start of August, GCT`s main commitments didn't commence until the school contracts started on the 18th of August. GCT managed to acquire a raft of contracts for school services mainly in the Bearsden, Milngavie and Bishopbriggs area. From the company's point of view this was fortunate as not all the buses had been repainted into GCT livery by the start of August. Indeed several buses were noted working the school contracts with their fronts and rears in GCT livery and their sides still carrying SBL livery and fleetnames. Examples noted at the time being GLA 5/6/11– 3/15– 8/24/31– 4/6/7. Transferred in after the start of operations were GLA 38– 40 which had been LA 775/951/2 with SBL. It took a while, but by February 1994 all the buses in this unit wore full GCT livery.

The company continued to expand during 1994 and SBL continued to be the main source of the new buses. That is new to GCT and not hot off the production line. GLA 41/2 arrived in March and by August GLA 43– 9 were in the fleet, however during June the first Atlantean , GLA 25, was withdrawn. Not only was GCT a proving ground for new staff, but also a shunting ground for older stock that was getting past its best. One notable old timer that joined

Standard length former Busways Atlanteans were few and far between with both SBL and GCT. GLA 32 was one and is seen in West Nile Street in September 1994. (B Ridgway)

the fleet from SBL during the summer of 1994 was LA 664. Prior to joining the fleet it had been repainted in 1960s style GCT livery to mark the centenary of municipal transport in Glasgow. The first former SBL Atlantean to retain its SBL fleetnumber (and not the last) the bus was supposed to be a regular performer on service 100, but seemed to spend a fair amount of time in Milngavie taking school kids to Douglas Academy.

In December 1994 GLA 2 was transferred on loan back to SBL with LA 1034 going to GCT in return. This subsequently became a regular occurrence and on more than one occasion I can recall seeing ex Nottingham Atlanteans operating SBL route 20, Drumchapel to East Kilbride, in full GCT livery.

The S.B. Holdings Group was still acquiring second-hand Atlanteans and in early 1995 it was rumoured that VET 606S and WAG 379X were to become GLA 50/1 with GCT and the company even had WAG 379X repainted in GCT livery. In the event both of these buses joined the Kelvin Central subsidiary without ever becoming part of the GCT fleet. A second Atlantean, GLA 11, was withdrawn in April 1995, although the company was still expanding. Former SBL Atlanteans were continuing to join the fleet, with GLA 50– 8 arriving in July 1995 when a new base was set up within Parkhead Garage and these were soon followed by LA 1043/ 1136/40/2– 4/7/8/50– 2, which arrived on loan from SBL at the same time. In the end all bar the last four buses would also join the fleet in January 1996, but the real interest was that although the first four buses received GCT livery, they also retained their SBL fleetnumbers.

1996 was the year when all things Atlantean went ballistic within GCT. Although accident damage had claimed GLA 47 in February of that year, over the next few months 17 Atlanteans were to be withdrawn as they became life expired, the buses concerned being GLA 9/10/2/4/5/7 /8/20/4/39/40/5/57/8 and LA 1136/40 1142. That GLA 10 was to get a temporary reprieve in June, when it returned to service, was neither here nor there. Replacements for the Atlanteans were beginning to arrive and some, considering the age profile of GCT until this point, were surprising to say the least. Two Volvo B6, new in 1994, that had been acquired by S.B. Holdings with the Loch Lomond Coaches business in April 1996, were repainted in GCT livery and put to work at the GCT unit in Larkfield Garage. From Kelvin Central came six more Volvo B6 and from SBL came hoards of cascaded Atlanteans. The influx of new stock to both KCB and SBL allowed stock to be redistributed within the group. In May 1996 alone LA 1148/50– 2/5– 9/63/6/8/9/75– 81/9 6/7/9/1221/32/64/8/9/76 joined GCT from SBL. Age of the buses wasn't the only concern for GCT in 1996 however. The traffic commissioner had carried out checks on the company's buses and 30 vehicles had been ordered off the road for a catalogue of mechanical defects. Faults included a bald tyre, loose propeller shaft blades, spring to axle bolts being loose and, in one case, a chassis that broke when touched by hand. Department of Transport examiner, Alan Campbell saying, ` A hammer easily passed through what

should have been solid metal and finger pressure could then be used to expand the hole.` Over and above these buses, GCT was ordered to carry out immediate repairs on a further 17 buses in its fleet. The upshot of all this activity by the commissioners resulted in GCT`s operating licence being reduced from 150 buses to 120 buses. It must be pointed out that none of these reports specifically mention Atlanteans, but the Atlantean was the backbone of the GCT fleet and it would be naïve in the least to believe the Atlanteans were receiving exemplarily care whilst the other buses were getting just in time maintenance. It is also worth noting that the traffic commissioners had been concerned by the maintenance of the company in 1994.

But it wasn't all doom and gloom for the GCT Atlantean. S.B.Holdings had been purchased by First Group during 1996 and the new owners had decided to paint all the buses that were being retained in a deep red livery. This resulted in a paint float fleet being set up in November 1996 and the GCT contingent initially consisted of LA 1175/7/9/89/1202 /8/15/6/21. By the New Year it was clear that the brush with the traffic commissioner had altered things. In January 1997 eight low floor East Lancs. bodied Dennis Darts, MD 1– 8, and two step entrance Plaxton bodied Darts, MD 9/10, entered GCT service from Knightswood Garage in the new First Glasgow red livery. The following month the GCT unit at Parkhead received former KCB Alexander bodied Volvo B10Ms, SV 420– 8, proof indeed that the Atlantean was on the way out at First Glasgow. Over the next few months major changes were afoot at GCT. In May, the head office moved from Knightswood Garage to Larkfield Garage and GCT buses had begun to appear with Greater Glasgow fleetnames. By June the unit at Parkhead Garage had ceased operations and in preparation for the closure of GCT, services began being transferred to Greater Glasgow or Kelvin Central Buses during September. By November, GCT had no Atlanteans left and the remaining buses had been corralled at Knightswood Garage. Although operations were scheduled to stop on January 3rd 1998 when the night buses were due to be transferred to Greater Glasgow, the reality is that from 29th November 1997 Greater Glasgow vehicles were maintaining the network on loan to GCT. So just over four years after its arrival, GCT was gone. A variety of vehicles had been operated, but the Atlantean had unquestionably been the backbone of operations.

On the next page is a table of all the Atlanteans known to have worked with GCT that carried GCT livery and gained GCT fleetnumbers. Also included is a list of the other Atlanteans transferred in from SBL that retained both SBL livery and fleetnumbers with the addition of a letter G for GCT, i.e. LA 1166 in the SBL fleet became GLA 1166 with GCT even though it retained SBL livery. Whilst every effort has been made to accurately list all these Atlanteans, it must be remembered that towards the end of Atlantean operation in Glasgow, the LAs were moving between units at a tremendous rate and it is possible that some buses operated at GCT and were not recorded.

GLA 1– 3 Leyland Atlantean AN68/1R Alexander `AL` H 45/31F
GLA 1 NGB 125M   GLA 2 OYS 162M   GLA 3 OYS 178M
Previously LA 757/65/81 with Strathclyde Buses

GLA 4– 10 Leyland Atlantean AN 68/1R East Lancs. H 45/33F
GLA 4 OTO 554M   GLA 7 OTO 567M   GLA 10 JAL 879N
GLA 5 OTO 561M   GLA 8 OTO 581M
GLA 6 OTO 566M   GLA 9 JAL 877N
Previously LA 1450– 6 with Strathclyde Buses

GLA 11/2 Leyland Atlantean AN68A/1R Alexander `AL` H 45/31F
GLA 11 JVK 234P   GLA 12 JVK 238P
Previously LA 1457/8 with Strathclyde Buses

GLA 13– 20 Ley. Atlantean AN68A/2R Alex. `AL` H 48/34F (GLA 13), H 48/33F (GLA 14/5/7– 20),
H 48/30F (GLA 16)
GLA 13 MVK 502R   GLA 16 MVK 512R   GLA 19 MVK 552R
GLA 14 MVK 506R   GLA 17 MVK 516R   GLA 20 MVK 567R
GLA 15 MVK 508R   GLA 18 MVK 526R
Previously LA 1459– 66 with Strathclyde Buses

GLA 21/2 Leyland Atlantean AN68A/1R Alexander `AL` H 45/31F
GLA 21 JVK 235P   GLA 22 JVK 236P
Previously LA 1467/8 with Strathclyde Buses

GLA 23– 30 Ley. Atlantean AN68A/2R Alex. `AL` H 48/33F (GLA 23– 5), H 49/37F (GLA 26– 30)
GLA 23 MVK 520R   GLA 26 VCU 305T   GLA 29 VCU 311T
GLA 24 MVK 527R   GLA 27 VCU 307T   GLA 30 VCU 313T
GLA 25 MVK 550R   GLA 28 VCU 308T
Previously LA 1469– 76 with Strathclyde Buses

GLA 31/2 Leyland Atlantean AN68A/1R Alexander `AL` H 45/31F
GLA 31 JVK 240P   GLA 32 JVK 243P
Previously LA 1477/8 with Strathclyde Buses

GLA 33– 37 Ley. Atlantean AN68A/2R Alex. `AL` H 48/34F (GLA 33), H 48/33F (GLA 34),
H 49/37F (GLA35-7)
GLA 33 MVK 503R   GLA 35 SCN 272S   GLA 37 UVK 296T
GLA 34 MVK 529R   GLA 36 UVK 293T
Previously LA 1479– 83 with Strathclyde Buses

GLA 38– 40 Leyland Atlantean AN68/1R Alexander `AL` H 45/31F
GLA 38 OYS 172M   GLA 39 KSU 827P   GLA 40 KSU 828P
Previously LA 775/951/2 with Strathclyde Buses

GLA 41– 58 Leyland Atlantean AN68A/1R Alexander `AL` H 45/31F
GLA 41 TGE 823R   GLA 46 TGE 832R   GLA 51 TGE 829R   GLA 56 TGG 747R
GLA 42 TGE 828R   GLA 47 TGE 837R   GLA 52 TGE 831R   GLA 57 TGG 748R
GLA 43 RUS 348R   GLA 48 TGE 839R   GLA 53 TGG 739R   GLA 58 TGG 750R
GLA 44 RUS 350R   GLA 49 TGG 736R   GLA 54 TGG 741R
GLA 45 TGE 827R   GLA 50 TGE 820R   GLA 55 TGG 746R
Previously LA 1104/09/1097/99/1108/13/18/20/21/01/10/12/24/26/31/32/33/35 with Strathclyde Buses

The following seven vehicles all gained GCT livery but retained their SBL fleetnumbers

Leyland Atlantean AN68A/1R Alexander `AL` H 45/31F
  LA 1043 MDS 706P   LA 1140 TGG 755R
  LA 1136 TGG 751R   LA 1142 TGG 757R

LA 664 gained 1960s style GCT livery but retained it's SBL fleetnumber

Leyland Atlantean AN68/1R Alexander `AL` H 45/29F
  LA 664 HGD 870L

The following Atlanteans, fleetnumbers only, are known to have been operated by GCT in SBL livery, retaining their SBL fleetnumbers :-
  LA 1034/1143/44/47/48/50– 52/54– 59/63/66/68/69/75– 81/83/85/89/96/97/99
  LA 1200– 02/04/08– 11/15/16/18/19/21/23/25/27– 29/31/32/35– 37/39/41– 53/56/61/64/68–70/72
  73/7 5/76/78/ 80/83/84/92/3
  LA 1310/21/23– 26/29/32/38/44/46– 48/50/53/54/57/75

As this image of GLA 42 in September `1994` proves, some of the Atlanteans in the GCT fleet were former SBL examples. Following up behind is a Kelvin Central (new to Central Scottish) Dennis Dominator, 1734, which soon after this photo was taken became part of the Strathclyde Bus Holdings fleet. (B. Ridgway)

Kelvin Central Buses, KCB

Towards the end of September 1994 S.B. Holdings purchased its chief competitor in the northern part of Glasgow, Kelvin Central Buses, KCB. That the former Corporation fleet had bought a former Scottish Bus Group subsidiary was ironic to say the least. In 1966 the SBG had offered to take the bus fleet off Glasgow Corporation's hands on a 30 year lease with Clydeside Omnibuses the rumoured name for the new operator. As history shows the deal foundered, but not before the Corporation had given a good deal of thought to the offer. Instead of former GCT buses working for the SBG, we had in the fullness of time former SPTE Atlanteans working from former SBG Garages at Airdrie, Cumbernauld, Kirkintilloch, Motherwell and Old Kilpatrick. Indeed the Kirkintilloch operations eventually transferred to Possilpark Garage and the operations at Old Kilpatrick were moved to Knightswood Garage in 1996. Without doubt the wheel had turned full circle and very few people had forecast that outcome at the onset of deregulation in 1986.

The effect of this consolidation could be seen by SBL`s market share in Glasgow jumping from 43% to 66%. Consolidation of the two fleets would also take place, but what would be in and what would be out? With both fleets having Ailsas, Metrobuses and Olympians, it was assumed that the Dominators, Fleetlines, Leopards, Nationals and Tigers might be culled. That the Dominators and Fleetlines went, wasn't much of a surprise, but the withdrawal of elderly ex-SBG Ailsas and their replacement by even older SBL Atlanteans did raise eyebrows.

23 of the oldest Atlanteans were transferred to Kelvin Central from SBL in February 1995 as 1901– 23 - an ironic choice of fleetnumbers as Kelvin had used the 19xx series for its Routemaster fleet that saw use on cross city routes in competition with SBL in the post deregulation years. But it wouldn't be Glasgow without a bit of confusion being involved! SBL had planned to send LA 1101/10/51/2 to KCB as 1910/1/ 21/2 but LA 1106/30/1030/1129 were actually dispatched. The 14 Atlanteans that were acquired second-hand, were given fleetnumbers 1924– 37 and all 37 Atlanteans were initially allocated to Cumbernauld,

By June 1995 LA 1138 had been repainted in KCB colours and had a new fleetnumber 1913.
Note the use of a plain window in the front lower nearside window instead of a vented window.
In the above image the bus had been temporarily transferred back to SBL. (B. Ridgway)

1901– 12/15– 7/20, and Kirkintilloch, 1913/4/8/9/21– 37. No sooner had some of the buses lost SBL livery than they were returned to Larkfield. The buses involved, 1907/9–11/13/5/6/8, worked SBL routes from Larkfield in KCB colours. The reason for this was that Kelvin had a pressing need for lowheight buses fitted with security screens for operation from Airdrie Garage. From the 7th May 1995 until July 1995 Leyland Olympians, LO 12/22/30/9/44/5/8/9, were temporary transferred to Kelvin in lieu of the Atlanteans.

It wasn't just the fleets that were being streamlined, the garages were undergoing a similar exercise. In 1995 the Kelvin garage at Kirkintilloch was moved into SBL`s Possilpark Garage. The Kelvin buses kept their red and cream livery and the garage operated as an out station of Old Kilpatrick garage. Not for long, however, as the operations at Old Kilpatrick were moved into Knightswood Garage the following year. Soon only Cumbernauld and Motherwell would remain of the ex KCB garages as consolidation of the SBL and KCB infrastructure began to take effect.

Roe bodied former South Yorkshire PTE Atlantean 1926, departs Buchannan Bus Station in June 1995. This dual door vehicle also carried the infamous signs on the centre door informing the public that the centre door was not in fact a door. (B. Ridgway)

Earlier in June 1995, Atlantean 1937, new to Hull in 1981, was caught leaving the same location on a local service to the north western suburbs of Glasgow. It is interesting to observe the differences in the body Roe produced for Hull when compared to the bus above. (B. Ridgway)

During 1995 much needed fleet renewal of the Kelvin fleet began on a large scale and whilst this didn't directly affect the Atlanteans, it did involve them. As KCB waited for the arrival of more Alexander `PS` bodied Volvo B10Ms, 2329– 88, in October 1995, SBL transferred LA 1153-5/68/1224/88/1303/57 to Motherwell Garage. Within a few days LA 1288/1303 were returned to SBL, but the rest of the buses remained to operate local services until the Volvos arrived the following month. The effects of the merger were beginning to be felt within SB Holdings and some of the youngest Atlanteans and oldest Olympians that were rendered surplus at SBL, were transferred to KCB. The Atlanteans mostly retained SBL livery, although two buses were put to work in SBL livery with KCB red fronts.

With the sale of S.B Holdings to First Group in 1996 the second-hand Atlanteans, 1924– 1937, were renumbered

LA 538– 51 and there was a large influx of new buses to KCB. Dennis Darts with various body types and Volvo B6 began to appear in the fleet. By the end of 1997 the writing was on the wall for the KCB Atlantean fleet. Out of a fleet of 497 buses only 13 were Atlanteans, the survivors being allocated to Knightswood, LA 539/47/ 9–51/1139, or reserve, LA 542/4– 6/8/1291/5. On the 28th May 1998 KCB was renamed First Glasgow No. 2 and the only Atlanteans left were LA 547/1139/1291/5. Of the original 37 Atlanteans LA 547(1933) and LA 1139 (1914) were the final examples in service with KCB when they were withdrawn in July 1998.

The table below contains details of the initial 37 Atlanteans sent to Kelvin Central Buses by SB Holdings in the spring of 1995.

1901– 7 Leyland Atlantean AN68/1R Alexander H45/31F

1901 NGB 125M	1903 OYS 162M	1905 OYS 178M	1907 OYS 188M
1902 NGB 128M	1904 OYS 174M	1906 OYS 184M	

1901/3/5 had previously been with GCT as GLA 1/2/3. All seven buses were new to GGPTE as LA 757/60/5/77/81/87/91

1908– 23 Leyland Atlantean AN68A/1R Alexander H45/31F

1908 MDS 697P	1912 TGG 752R	1916 TGG 756R	1920 TGG 750R
1909 MDS 712P	1913 TGG 753R	1917 TGG 737R	1921 MDS 693P
1910 TGE 825R	1914 TGG 754R	1918 TGG 738R	1922 TGG 744R
1911 TGG 745R 1	915 TGG 742R	1919 TGG 749R	1923 RUS 303R

All 16 buses new to GGPTE as LA 1034/49/1106/30/7/8/9/27/41/22/3/34/5/1030/1129/1052

1924 Leyland Atlantean AN68A/1R Roe H45/29D
1924 VET 606S

1925 Leyland Atlantean AN68A/1R Alexander H45/29D
1925 CWG 720V

1926/7 Leyland Atlantean AN68A/1R Roe H45/29D
1926 CWG 771V   1927 CWG 772V

1928/9 Leyland Atlantean AN68B/1R Marshall H45/29F
1928 JKW 319W   1929 JKW 320W

1930– 7 Leyland Atlantean AN68C/1R Roe H43/31F

1930 WAG 370X	1933 WAG 373X	1936 WAG 376X	1931 WAG 381X
1934 WAG 374X	1937 WAG 377X	1932 WAG 378X	1935 WAG 379X

During 1996 the fleet renumbering exercise was implemented throughout SB Holdings. Those Atlanteans between 1901 and 1923 that were still operational regained their original LA fleetnumber. 1924– 37 were allocated fleetnumbers LA 538– 51.

The following former Strathclyde Buses Atlanteans are also known to have operated with this subsidiary. As with GCT, due to the rapidity of fleet transfers the following list is what is known to have operated with KCB and may not represent all buses to have been operated.

LA 1043/1147/53– 5/68/92/1208/19/23– 5/28/34/7/43 /50/2/61/2/7/81/8/91– 5/1301/3/28/57/1406/1450– 3 LA 1243 came to KCB from GCT and it operated in SBL livery

with a KCB red front. LA 1281 was also put to work in this livery after its transfer from SBL.

LA 1450– 3 referred to above are the former Grampian examples that joined the fleet in May 1997 prior to their transfer to Greater Glasgow.

GLA 16/32/4/8 were transferred from the GCT Comlaw 313 fleet and retained GCT livery.

The Trainers

So you fancied driving a bus did you? You think because you like buses that driving one can't be that hard, eh? It can't be that hard, after all it's really just a long car with a bit of extra height, isn't it? If only it was, then bus companies wouldn't need to teach drivers (almost all of whom already hold a car licence) the intricacies of driving a bus. In the early seventies turnover in omo staff within GCT was running at between 30 and 50 % despite initiatives to increase staff numbers. The fact that bus companies use their oldest buses to train new drivers shows that learning to drive a bus is not a piece of cake and sadly most of the public look down on this undervalued skill with contempt. Leaving asides the public relations element of the job, a driver has to move a swaying mass of metal through often narrow streets whilst maintaining reasonable speed without hitting any street furniture and, more importantly, without endangering the lives of his passengers or anyone in the path of his bus. In GCT days, training of new drivers took place in withdrawn buses from the main fleet.

When LA 1 became the first Atlantean trainer in April 1973, the standard GCT training bus was the Leyland PD 2 Titan. Like the Titan fleet before them, the majority of Atlantean trainers would retain their fleetnumbers from the main fleet. Fitted with small `L` plates and an advert for driver recruitment on the between decks side panels, LA 1 served the training school for just over a year before it was retired. Until late 1975 both Titans and Atlanteans were being sent to the training school. Some vehicles served for only a few months before withdrawal, whilst the majority spent several years in the training fleet. The longevity of some of the Atlantean trainers can be seen in that some of the recruits from early eighties lasted to within a year or two of the withdrawal of Atlanteans from the service fleet.

The more knowledgeable Glasgow enthusiast will recall the numerous cut and paste jobs that afflicted the Atlantean trainers. Early 1975 saw the destination screens removed from some of the buses, whilst others had large white warning posters placed over the screens. A more radical alteration took place in September 1976 when LA 201 had a seat for the instructor and an extra off side window inserted after the stairwell over the front offside axle was removed, LA 297 and LA 318 also being similarly treated.

After being transferred to the driving school, LA 201 had a small window inserted behind the diver's cab. (David.G. Wilson)

By 1979 with the fleet rapidly heading towards 100% omo operation , there was naturally a surplus of conductors who could be retrained as drivers. This led to LA 305 and LA 322 being sold to Ritchie (PSV Training) of Glasgow who used the buses to help with the training of PTE drivers. It would be wrong to assume that a shortage of PTE trainers was requiring the use of outside contractors; far from it, in August 1979 there were 28 Atlanteans working for the training school. It is hardly surprising that by the following March staff shortages had fallen from 20% to just 6%, the retraining of conductors as drivers being cited as one of the reasons for this reduction. Indeed such were the numbers of conductors wishing to become drivers that by now the PTE halted recruitment of drivers for the first time in almost fifty years. Driving Inspectors rendered surplus were sent to work for the Traffic Research and Development Section to undertake census and survey work. By July 1980 there were 29 buses in the training fleet as follows :- LA 220/30/6/54/8/9/65/79/90/4/5/7– 9/303/4/8/ 18/ 67/680/2 /4/9/700/18/37/41/2/5.

Towards the end of the seventies, surplus dual door Atlanteans from the main fleet were a regular sight at the training school and for the first time since LA 201 in 1976 an Atlantean trainer underwent a major rebuild when LA 682 appeared during October 1979 with its front door removed. In its place was a window and on the platform a seat for the instructor had been inserted, the centre exit remained in situ and the upper decks was sealed off. These features subsequently became standard on regular members of the training fleet, as did the all over white livery that the bus was finished in.

Only 12 buses, LA 680/2/97/8/700/10/9/41/2/5/61/85,

remained as trainers by the end of 1987, several AN 68s having returned to the service fleet as a result of Strathclyde Buses having to reorganise to counter the effects of deregulation. Towards the end of the eighties some of the training buses began to appear with orange blocks on their previously all white livery and it gave the impression of being an all over advert for driver training and recruitment.

By May 1996 the training fleet had begun to receive former Kelvin Central Leyland National 1s in place of the Atlanteans. The fleet comprising LA 680/2/97/710 and Nationals SN 11/3/7/22/3/30 with the Atlanteans bowing out of service in October of that year. The Nationals however were to have a short life in the training fleet, by August 1997 SN 11/3/7/30 were out of use. Their replacements were yet more Atlanteans, this time LA 1396/9/1400/2/3 being employed with LA 1416/7 following along the next month. LA 1396 was put to work in a new training bus livery of all over First Glasgow red with a between decks yellow band, the shade of red being the same as that applied to the buses seeing passenger service. LA 1399 was one Atlantean that initially was used in plain all over red before gaining the yellow band at a later date. LA 1402/16/7 were put to work in SBL orange and black livery with small `L` plates applied below the front windscreen before the buses succumbed to the inevitable red paint brush. As well as having their top decks sealed, with the seats still in place, most of these buses had their front destination boxes panelled over, although LA 1416 merely had its destination box painted over. Breaking with tradition, these buses lost their previous fleetnumbers and were renumbered T1– 7 for their new duties.

Considering the abuse that training buses take, it is remarkable that some have survived into preservation,

LA 698 with panelled over destination display and wearing the less than inspiring
all white training livery sits in Saint Enoch Square. (David.G.Wilson)

the best known being LA 1. LA 697 was saved from the scrapyard and is currently undergoing restoration, having been rebuilt to its original two door formation. It is believed that the bus, which appeared at the Glasgow Bus Museum open day in 2001 in all over white livery, is to be restored to GGPTE livery. LA 1416 has also been secured for preservation and is heading back into SBL livery, LA 1399 on the otherhand remained in withdrawn condition with some work done on its electrics. This bus has since been sold to an owner in Belgium where its current condition is unknown. LA 1396/9/1400/ 2/16/7 initially passed from First Glasgow to Glasgow preservationist Michael Roulston. Whilst the fate of some of these buses has been highlighted above, LA 1402 was broken up at the GBM`s Bridgeton site as a source of spares. LA 1396/1417 were disposed of to Dunsmore of Larkhall for scrap in the spring of 2003. LA 1400`s remains were last seen in Possilpark Garage in the summer of 2003 when Michael Roulston had his collection

of buses stored there: its current fate is unknown. If it hasn't already been scrapped it almost certainly will be soon. That leaves just LA 1403 (T5) as the very last Glasgow Atlantean to see active service. It was still seeing use on route training duties until the autumn of 2002. The bus remained on the official fleetlist of First Glasgow despite spending the remainder of its life in Glasgow parked over a pit in Knightswood Garage, even gaining a tax disc valid until September 2003. This possibly explains why this inactive vehicle received a First Group national fleetnumber, on paper anyway. I visited the bus at the end of May that year with the possibility of acquiring the bus for preservation. Sadly the bus was in a poor state and would have required a lot of cash to restore it. Unsurprisingly, after being moved to Larkfield Garage and a further period of storage, the bus was finally dispatched to Dunmore's at Larkhall for scrap. Below is a table of all the Atlanteans known to have been transferred to the training fleet.

LA 1	LA 130	LA 227	LA 282	LA 303	LA 684	LA 737	LA 803	LA 1396 (T1)
LA 14	LA 150	LA 230	LA 287	LA 304	LA 697	LA 738	LA 810	LA 1399 (T2)
LA 20	LA 152	LA 236	LA 288	LA 308	LA 698	LA 741	LA 811	LA 1400 (T3)
LA 45	LA 161	LA 254	LA 290	LA 318	LA 699	LA 742	LA 812	LA 1402 (T4)
LA 49	LA 174	LA 258	LA 294	LA 354	LA 700	LA 745	LA 813	LA 1403 (T5)
LA 50	LA 191	LA 259	LA 295	LA 367	LA 710	LA 759		LA 1416 (T6)
LA 105	LA 192	LA 263	LA 296	LA 479	LA 713	LA 761		LA 1417 (T7)
LA 107	LA 198	LA 265	LA 297	LA 480	LA 714	LA 768		
LA 109	LA 201	LA 267	LA 298	LA 489	LA 718	LA 771		
LA 110	LA 220	LA 273	LA 299	LA 680	LA 719	LA 780		
LA 117	LA 225	LA 279	LA 301	LA 682	LA 720	LA 785		

T7, or LA 1417 as it was known in old money, waits to meet its end on a dull March day in 2003 at Dunmore's in Larkhall. (Author)

 # Life after Glasgow

Until the early eighties, the number of ex Glasgow Atlanteans sold for further use was relatively small. Several operators did take them, however, and two of these companies were Allander Coaches of Milngavie and Whippet Coaches of Fenstanton. The buses usually gave a few years service to their new owners, but the most common destination for withdrawn buses was still the scrapyard. This changed noticeably in the early eighties when the PTE suddenly had large numbers of panoramic bodied Atlanteans to dispose of. The reasons for the disposal of these buses has already been made clear, so any operator purchasing one of these Atlanteans would know the problems associated with the body. Clearly some of the new owners were prepared to carry out their own rectification work as some of the Atlanteans disposed of at this time remained active until mid 2005.

Ulsterbus was the first large operator to show an interest in the defective AN68s when it purchased eight buses in February 1982. Prior to delivery, the buses were repainted into the Ulsterbus livery of all over blue with white roof at Larkfield Bus Works and the security screens were also removed from the buses at this time. The buses then were delivered to Ulster via the Stranrear to Larne ferry. In total Ulsterbus bought four batches of Atlanteans from the PTE and the buses were used on school contracts all over the province. Depots known to have operated the buses included Coleraine, Criagavon, Londonderry, Magherafelt and Omagh. In line with normal Ulsterbus practice for school buses, several were delicensed during the summer school holidays before being reactivated for the new school term.

The buses had a varied history with Ulsterbus, some buses, LA 821/55, gained fleetnumbers with their new owner despite being purchased as a source of spares. Equally unfortunate was the former LA 976 which entered service from Omagh garage on the 1st March 1983. The bus was destroyed by an incendiary device the next day when a terrorist attack was executed on the garage. The former LA 853 being sent to Omagh as its direct replacement. LA 915/55/1005 all saw use on private hires from the Short Strand Depot of Citybus. For those not familiar with Ulster, Citybus is the sister company of Ulsterbus and operated local bus services within Belfast prior to the formation of Translink. LA 991 was one of the earliest withdrawals when it was disposed from the reserve fleet in December 1986, but LA 996 kept going until May 1991. LA 989 found further use with an Ulster education institute and didn't go for scrap until 1998. Whilst Ulsterbus bought more Atlanteans from other sources including Lothian, it never returned for any more buses to Strathclyde. Listed below is a table detailing the 25 Atlanteans sold by Strathclyde PTE to Ulsterbus.

The impending threat of deregulation brought rationalisation to the Strathclyde fleet and amongst the redundant Atlanteans, 21 were sold to London Country Bus Services in 1986 for use on London Transport contracts. Ironically, as this was happening, both Clydeside and Kelvin Scottish were buying surplus AEC Routemasters

Ulsterbus Fleetnumber	Strathclyde Fleetnumber	Registration Number	Ulsterbus Fleetnumber	Strathclyde Fleetnumber	Registration Number
First batch, delivered March 1982			Third batch, delivered November 1982 to April 1983		
955	LA 1005	MDS 668P	969	LA 973	KSU 849P
956	LA 1006	MDS 669P	970	LA 976	KSU 852P
957	LA 989	KSU 865P	971	LA 921	JGA 203N
958	LA 991	KSU 867P	972	LA 955	KSU 831P
959	LA 993	KSU 869P	973	LA 915	JGA 197N
960	LA 996	KSU 872P	974	LA 844	SGA 727N
961	LA 997	KSU 873P	962	LA 999	KSU 875P
Second batch, delivered September 1982			Fourth batch, delivered December 1984		
963	LA 929	JUS 776N	975	LA 802	OYS 199M
964	LA 898	HGG 247N	976	LA 804	OYS 201M
965	LA 851	GGG 303N	977	LA 808	OYS 205M
966	LA 853	GGG 305N	978	LA 819	RGB 600M
967	LA 855	GGG 307N	979	LA 821	RGB 602M
968	LA 856	GGG 308N			

from London Buses to compete against Strathclyde Buses. The Atlanteans were refurbished and painted at Larkfield Bus Works prior to their dispatch to England. The green livery essentially being to standard National Bus Company layout with a light green band where a white one was usually positioned. The buses involved, LA 827/8/30/1/5/6/9/41/6/59/63/80/1/9/90/9/910/24/66/84/7 becoming AN 306– 26 respectively with London Country. A few buses saw use in early June 1986 at Dorking, Leatherhead and Reigate garages, prior to their temporary withdrawal for further modifications. From 21st June the buses were put to work from Hatfield, AN 307/9/11/2/6/21/3/6, Hemel Hempstead, AN 310/5, and Saint Albans, AN 306/8. A further ten buses, AN 327–36, arrived in August when LA 766/73/ 89/803/10–3/8/40, made the trip south.

In early September 1986, London Country was reorganised into four smaller operating units. Each new unit retaining London Country in their title with the appropriate North West (LCNW), North East (LCNE), South East (LCSE) or South West (LCSW) added. At the time of the split the 31 Atlanteans were owned by the following companies :-

LCNE AN 306– 9/11/2/6/21/3/6
LCNW AN 310/5
LCSE AN 313/4/7/9/20/2/4/5/7/32/3/6
LCSW AN 318/28– 31/4/5

The buses allocated to LCSE, later renamed Kentish Bus, were allocated to Swanley Junction for operation of LRT route 51 and were later renumbered into the 6xx

series by Kentish Bus, but not before the former LA 985 was purchased from Smith of Aberdeen as AN 337.

The 32 Atlanteans purchased by London Country did not have a long life in London. By the end of 1987 all of the LCNE examples, with the exception of withdrawn AN 312, were based at Hatfield. The following February all 10 buses at Hatfield were redundant. The LRT contracts that LCNE had needed the buses for, routes 292/8/313, had been lost. Whilst crew and engineering staff shortages played a part in the contracts being lost, the condition of the ex Strathclyde Atlanteans were also cited as a reason. Wigley, dealer, of Carlton took AN 308/9/11/6/21 as well as the remains of AN 312, although not all of the buses went for scrap, AN 306/7 being sold to Stuarts of Hyde, AN 323 was sold to Partridge Coaches of Hadleigh and AN 326, the real LA 1000, went to East Yorkshire. Kentish Bus also rationalized its Atlanteans in the spring of 1988 with the sale of AN 313/4/9/20/2/4/5/32/3/7 to Liverline of Liverpool. The final two examples at Kentish Bus, AN 317/27 lasted until June 1989.

The last of the 32 Atlanteans to see passenger service in London were withdrawn by LCSW towards the end of 1989, however AN 330 was converted by the company into a tree lopper. In a strange twist of fate, South Yorkshire Atlantean 1720, CWG 720V, was loaned to London & Country at the end of 1990 when the operator was waiting for new vehicles to be delivered, this bus later becoming 1925 with Kelvin Central. Once again some of the buses found new owners, AN 329/31/5 being sold to the Bee Line Buzz Company as

The former LA 810 had become AN 331 with London Country when it was photographed at Morden Station operating LRT contract service 293. (D. Rowe)

675– 7 for use on services in the Manchester area. Their service life here was to be short as all had been withdrawn by the spring of 1991.

Rennies of Dunfermline is perhaps the best known amongst Scottish enthusiasts for buying ex Strathclyde Atlanteans, although the company sourced a sizeable Atlantean fleet from several companies. Painted mainly cream with two red bands, the buses were put to work on a network of services around Dunfermline that the operator had commenced in the post deregulation era. The earliest ex SBL AN68s comprised LA 706/16/22/32 /43/8/9/65/9/ 86/815/77/9/1014/46/69, whilst the summer of 1988 would see another 52 Atlanteans purchased from SBL. Only 18 buses were kept for further use whilst 10 unused buses, LA 1013/40/1/53/66/77/88/9 /96 /1198 were sold to Liverline. The remaining buses, LA 711/51/68/72/6/82/4/92/4/801/6/ 14/72/900/1015/27/ 32/5/55/63– 5/7/8, were swiftly sold to Blythswood, a Glasgow dealer.

As noted earlier in the chapter, Liverline of Liverpool also purchased Strathclyde Atlanteans, 25 in total. Liverline commenced operations on the 11th April 1988 using a white and pale blue livery with a dark blue skirt. The company purchased 10 Atlanteans from Kentish Bus, one time LA 811/2/41/6/89/90/910/66/84/5, plus LA 935 which was bought from Swanbrook of Cheltenham for spares prior to operations starting. The summer of 1988 saw the 10 Atlanteans arrive from Rennies and in February 1989 LA 779/88/1045/1105 came from SBL. The final two Atlanteans, LA 841/966, were withdrawn towards the end of

1990. In common with the Atlanteans at London Country, the buses also caused concern here. This really shouldn't have been a shock considering no major structural repairs had been carried out on their panoramic bodies.

Thereafter, the sale of stock by SBL declined to negligible levels until 1996. The Glasgow Atlantean was now in decline, but with SBL now part of First Group that didn't mean the end for surplus SBL stock. A shock departure was LA 1142/60/74/44/76 being disposed of to First Greater Manchester as 4801– 5. The transfer was odd as not only was Greater Manchester disposing of younger Atlanteans from its own fleet, but the ex SBL buses were all Alexander bodied and non standard when compared to the Atlanteans in the Manchester fleet. LA 1142/4/76 were transferred from GCT with the other two coming from the SBL fleet. Preparation work was carried out at Larkfield Garage, although in the end this didn't really matter. Within months most of the buses had been sold for scrap by Greater Manchester to the Barnsley dealers. Only 4804 managed to avoid this fate, being sold to Rumbletums of Leigh for use as a playbus.

One other significant sale in the summer of 1997 was of LA 1191/82/24/41 within First Group to Welsh subsidiary Brewers. The South Wales operator allocated fleetnumbers 950– 3 to the buses. In September, LA 1261/1322/ 1287/1324 left Glasgow heading for South Wales as 954/62/61/955. 950/1/3 were cannibalised in Wales without being used by Brewers, although the buses were renumbered 930– 2 before this happened. The others were put to work in a variety of

Once LA 810's career in London was over, the bus later saw life with Bee Line in the Manchester area. Here she is seen in Piccadilly Gardens in Manchester city centre. (D. Rowe)

liveries. 952 got Brewers livery, 955 received South Wales livery and 954/61/2 were put to work in SBL livery. 955 which had short bay windows inserted in the lower deck of its panoramic body was later transferred within First Group to Western National in July 1999 and in 2000 was sold to Hoare of Chepstow. 952 was the last of the eight Atlanteans transferred to Wales to remain operational with First Cymru, as the Brewers and South Wales operations were later renamed.

The former LA 907 and LA 927 lay over between school duties at Don's yard in Dunmow, Essex in September 2004. Incredibly, these buses spent almost three quarters of their working life of thirty years with this family run business. They are a testament to the care and attention that buses sometimes can only get by being part of a small fleet. (Author)

A reunion of preserved former Don's of Dunmow Atlanteans occurred at the Bus World Museum in September 2005. LA 927 contrasts with former Grahams of Paisley Atlantean L1. It is planned to repaint LA 927 into PTE 2 livery whilst the missing Atlantean, LA 907, was also purchased for preservation by enthusiasts in the North East of England and has been repainted into GGPTE livery. (Author)

You say orange, I say red, Strathclyde red

Throughout the forty years of Atlantean operation in Glasgow, the buses wore a variety of liveries. LA 1 was unique amongst Atlanteans in wearing the 1950s style livery of cream uppers and roof, bus green between the decks, cream lower windows and orange lower panels with maroon wheels.

By the time LA 2 arrived in 1962, the livery had been simplified to bus green over the upper half of the bus, orange on the lower panels and saloon windows with a cream band separating the two colours, except for the front, with the wheels remaining maroon. LA 2 was unique amongst LA 2-716 in having a cream band above the driver's windscreen, although this was subsequently removed. This simplified livery was introduced to allow spray painting of the buses to take place at Larkfield Bus Works. The main advantage

of this move being that buses could be repainted every two years instead of every four years when they were hand painted. Concerns with the new livery became apparent in late 1964 when 21 buses, including Atlanteans LA 24/7 and 188, and a trolleybus were outshopped in an experimental reverse livery. Whilst placing the darkest colour, green, at the bottom of the bus made operational sense, the public were not taken with the idea and within a month they had all been repainted back into ' right way round' GCT livery. With the exception of the red dot to highlight 'omo' buses the livery descended into a period of stability until the arrival of the first AN 68 Atlanteans in 1972, some of which had Brunswick green applied to the wheels instead of the traditional maroon.

The Greater Glasgow Passenger Transport Authority,

In the upper picture taken at the Bus Works, LA 1 carrying the spray painted GCT livery has been shunted whilst awaiting further attention. Parked next to it is Daimler D 189. (A.J. Douglas)

LA 188, bottom, carrying the short lived reverse livery, leads a line of buses, including a Daimler, all heading for the Midland Street terminus that was located underneath Central Station. (A.J. Douglas)

GGPTA, was formed in 1972 in advance of GGPTE taking control the following year. GGPTA consisted of four members who were nominated by the Secretary of State for Scotland, as well as councillors who represented the various councils within the GGPTA boundary. Essentially, GGPTE`s remit was to carry out the wishes of the GGPTA.

When GGPTE assumed control of the bus fleet in June 1973, things initially continued pretty much as before with LA 696– 716 being delivered to the new PTE in GCT livery. Mr Cox, the new Director General, wanted a new livery and to this end a team was formed to undertake such a task. Over at Larkfield Bus Works, Alan Westwell had fibreglass bus sides produced, these being approximately two feet long by ten inches high. Around sixty basic liveries were applied to these moulds on a progressive basis, each new livery being assessed by the team on whether they were similar to other operators within the PTE area. The large number of SBG buses operating for a host of companies in the Glasgow area, precluding liveries that were dominated by one colour like red, blue or green. It is reported that Mr Cox favoured a blue based livery, essentially Edinburgh's livery with blue instead of madder. The PTA, dominated by Glasgow councillors wanted to preserve Glasgow's traditional green and orange colours. A compromise was reached with Mr Cox stating that whatever livery was chosen, it should have white roof and upper deck windows and white lower deck windows. If green and orange were to be used, they had to be different British Standard shades of the colours the Corporation had previously used. Mr Westwell felt that the

operating conditions in Glasgow weren't suited to the large scale use of a light colour like white, which has additional cleaning costs associated to its use if a good image is to be presented to the public. His preferred option, from an engineering viewpoint, was to have a darker colour on the roof. Mr Cox, however, overruled this, sticking with his preferred large scale use of white along with green and yellow.

Prior to the adoption of the livery, three newly delivered Atlanteans, LA 697– 699, were repainted in varying shades of white, yellow and green at the Bus Works in June 1973. Presumably one of these buses wore the new PTE livery, but as no photographs have come to light, it is impossible to be sure. The new livery applied goldcup yellow between the decks, Verona green on the lower panels, these two areas being separated by Mr Cox's white areas with the Brunswick green wheels from the last GCT Atlanteans being incorporated into the PTE livery. The new livery was bright, to say the least, but its similarity to the colours of one of Glasgow's major football teams also made it contentious. Leyland Titan PD 2 L 118 was the first bus repainted into the new livery, with LA 697—700/3 being the first Atlanteans in the new livery and LA 717 being the first bus delivered in the new colours. The unveiling of the new livery came on the 6th July when two Atlanteans, LA 700 and LA 703, were put on public display with one bus being sent to George Square and one to Saint Enoch Square. It is interesting that none of the buses involved in the livery experiments were used in the unveiling. Early repaints into the new livery did not carry fleetnames and fleetnumbers were silver digits on

LA 266, carrying the first PTE livery, heads across Glasgow Bridge on its way to Darnley on the southern edge of the city. The northern terminus of service 57 at this time was officially Radnor Street, although in reality it was Clayslaps Road. (David.G Wilson)

a black background mounted on a metal rectangle. When LA 751 was displayed to the public at the Kelvin Hall Show in November 1973 it carried the `GG` symbol and it had a new style of fleetnumber plate. The front and side plates had a white background with black digits. The rear plate had black digits mounted on a yellow background. Whilst this style of plate was fitted as standard from LA 799 and was eventually retrofitted to LA 651 upwards, buses LA 752– 798 reverted to GCT silver transfers for fleetnumbers. The final operational bus in GCT livery was LA 490 which was repainted into GGPTE livery in January 1976.

The livery then descended into a period of stability over the next seven years with only the addition of the `Trans - Clyde` legend below the `GG` symbol in October 1979 occurring during this period. Alan Westwell`s return to the PTE as its third Director General in November 1979, however, was to have an impact on the livery. The white parts of the livery that the new Director General had disliked back in 1973 were soon to be removed. In September 1980 LA 795 emerged after work on its panoramic body with a deeper shade of yellow applied between decks. It is believed that the durability of the colour was the reason for this. At the same time all buses emerging from repaint were carrying the `Trans - Clyde` fleetname only, the `GG` having been dispensed with. The days of the first PTE livery were now numbered. The following Atlanteans were delivered in PTE 1 livery, LA 717– 1409 and LA 1412– 1421.

Just as Glaswegians would complain about waiting half an hour for a bus and then three arrived together, the same applied to the liveries. Besides the livery variation on LA

795, two new liveries were also unveiled during September 1980. PTE 2 livery was a simplification of the first scheme. The goldcup was carried over the upper deck windows and roof , the Verona green was extended to include the lower deck windows and the white now consisted of a narrow band separating the two main colours. The overall effect was similar to the unsuccessful livery that was experimented with in late 1964. A new addition to the livery was a black skirt that started behind the front axle and also included the area around the fuel filler cap. Mr Westwell felt this was a useful addition from the point of disguising dirt and helping to maintain the buses in good appearance. Not every bus repainted in PTE 2 livery received this black skirt, LA 938/1041 and LA 1138 being amongst the buses to initially escape this treatment. One bus, LA 873, received an amalgam of PTE1 and PTE 2 livery with the top half of the bus receiving all over yellow and the lower half of the bus remaining in the GGPTE livery. The bus remained in this livery until it was withdrawn in 1982. Very few Atlanteans were delivered in PTE 2 livery, only LA 1422– 1435/7/8, the absence of LA 1436 from this list , owing to it entering service in an all over advert for Strathclyde Regional Council's ` Fostering` service. These new vehicles also introduced a small livery variation in that buses painted at Alexanders had the offside area around the stairwell painted half white/ half Verona green, whereas buses painted at the Bus Works had this area completely green.

September 1980 also saw the debut of the third PTE livery when Leyland Olympian LO 1 appeared at the Motor

As this image of LA 640 in Saint Enoch Square shows, early AN 68 Atlanteans without engine shrouds, carried the second PTE livery; indeed LA 637 carried PTE 3 livery. Note the continued use of GCT silver transfers for fleetnumbers. (D.G. Wilson)

Show in Birmingham wearing a livery of yellow upper half, black lower deck windows and green lower deck panels with a black skirt and black fuel cap surrounds. The first Atlanteans to wear this scheme were LA 1410/1 which arrived in this livery in November 1980. A small livery variation within these two buses was the continuation of the black skirt forward of the front axle to the edge of the front dash panel on LA 1411 but not on LA 1410. LA 1439–49 were the only Atlanteans to be delivered in this scheme and in common with all subsequent LA repaints into PTE 3 livery, the black skirt was confined to aft of the front axle. Just to confuse matters further a variant of PTE 3 livery appeared on LA 947 in the spring of 1981 wearing primrose yellow on the upper half and a deeper shade of green on the lower panels with black lower deck window surrounds and skirt. This Knightswood based bus was withdrawn during 1982 still carrying this livery.

The fourth and final PTE livery made its debut on Atlanteans in April 1982 when cut down Atlantean SA 1 was unveiled. The livery consisting of all over orange with the black window surrounds, skirt and fuel cap surround being retained from the third stage livery. In a city like Glasgow where football and religious beliefs often mix uncomfortably close the idea of orange buses was an interesting concept. It must be remembered that the Underground trains and the trains on the PTE sponsored rail network around Glasgow were also being repainted into the orange scheme. The PTE came up with an interesting solution to the problem of a colour that had been known as 'hot orange' when it had first appeared on the Underground trains. Reflecting the fact that the Underground trains were based in Govan the livery then became ' Govan Orange'. Those with a

reasonable knowledge of Glasgow's geography would realise that to a minority of the city's populace this was worse than having orange buses and trains. Showing that it had mastered the art of wordplay, the PTE announced that this orangest of orange colours wasn't orange at all, oh no it was red, Strathclyde red to be exact. Regardless of monikers, the livery was initially confined to inter station buses. Soon after, it was decided that the livery should be used on all rail associated services with LA 1359 being the first double decker to wear the orange for use on service 94, Renfrew Street– Crookston Castle, which replaced the withdrawn Glasgow Central– Kilmacolm rail service within the city boundary. Early repaints into this scheme were given ' Strathclyde' fleetnames before the more familiar ' Strathclyde Transport' and stylised map of the region became established. Just to confuse issues further LA 1138 in PTE 2 livery and LA 1249 in PTE 3 livery gained the new logo. At this point in time it was understood that the Strathclyde red livery would be confined to the single deckers and the five double deckers operating rail related services. By June 1983 this policy was out the window with Councillor Cannell, the Vice Chairman of the Highways and Transportation Committee, announcing that the orange and black would be adopted as standard as, ' It had gone down well,' and , ' nor would it cost tax payers money,'. An interesting statement as repaints into the fourth PTE livery were not being confined to buses undergoing overhaul at Larkfield Bus Works. The effect of this constant rebranding of image was confusing for the public, it was possible for a garage to supply buses in four different PTE liveries to the one route as well as advertising liveried buses, and if your local garage was Larkfield you might even get a City Tour

LA 1411, carrying PTE 3 livery, heads past Shawlands Station. The application of black paint ahead of the front axle was not used in standard Atlantean repaints into PTE 3 livery. (D.G.Wilson)

bus thrown in as well.

It might seem funny to the bus enthusiast who has a knowledge of bus companies that the man in the street does not possess, but to the public it must have felt that some routes had several different operators on them. Despite this multiplicity of liveries, efforts to remove earlier liveries were not rapid. LA 683 sauntered along in PTE 1 livery until August 1984, whilst LA 803 was believed to be the last bus in the second PTE livery in January 1985, although by this time the bus was with the driving school. It isn't clear when the last bus in PTE 3 livery was repainted but by September 1985 there were no serviceable buses left in any of the first three PTE schemes.

In June 1986 the company was renamed Strathclyde Buses Limited, SBL, in preparation for the deregulation of local bus services throughout the UK in October 1986. There was no change to the livery, but the fleetnames were changed to Strathclyde's Buses and the legal lettering reflected the move of the head office to Larkfield Garage in Victoria Road. A small alteration to the livery throughout the fleet in the autumn of 1988 was the repainting of the wheels from black to orange. The livery for the main fleet then remained unaltered until First Group bought SBL in 1996.

The formation of GCT in August 1993 saw the return of green, black and yellow buses to Glasgow's streets. As with the third stage PTE livery, yellow covered the upper half of the bus and the green used on the lower panels, a darker

LA 1447, top, was an early recipient of PTE 4 livery for its use on the rail replacement service 94 to Crookston Castle. This service started, following the withdrawal of the rail service to Kilmacolm. (A.J. Douglas)

As LA 1324 demonstrates at Govan Bus Station, apart from the fleetname and later the colour of the wheels, SBL and SPTE livery were the same. The stylized map of the region was later dropped by SBL; however, the additional fleetname below the front windscreen became standard. (David.G.Wilson)

shade than used by the PTE, had similarities to the shade used on LA 947. Separating the two colours was a narrow black band.

The other fleet in the Strathclyde Buses Holdings group, Kelvin Central Buses, had been purchased in late 1994 and by February 1995 Atlanteans were being sent to the new subsidiary from SBL. Painted in the then current KCB livery of allover bright red with a narrow cream band just above the lower deck windows, the buses had a similarity to the livery adopted by Fife Scottish in the mid eighties.

With the sale of SBL to First Group in 1996, the operating name of the company was changed to Greater Glasgow. Whilst the majority of Atlanteans would run until withdrawal in whatever livery they wore at the time of the takeover, 10 Atlanteans were repainted into Greater Glasgow allover red. A much deeper, and boring, shade

was applied than the red that been used on the Kelvin Central Buses. The Atlanteans to receive this scheme were former Grampian examples LA 1450– 3 and local examples LA 1313/95/1419/24/40/3. Greater Glasgow fleetnames in grey and outlined in white were applied on the lower deck between the axles as well as to the front and rear of each bus. The resident examples losing their GGPTE inspired fleetnumber plates, grey transfers taking their place. As part of the preparations for the Atlantean running day on June 8th 1998, LA 1440 gained white `First` fleetnames and a white ` Glasgow` local identity transfer below the driver's cab window. The Atlanteans that retained SBL livery had a lick of orange paint applied over their Strathclyde's Buses fleetnames and grey Greater Glasgow fleetnames applied in their place. It certainly wasn't tidy bit it was in keeping with the Glasgow way of doing things.

The positioning of the stairwell on the nearside was an unusual feature that was found on some batches of Busways Atlanteans. GLA 23 is seen in Renfield Street, note the protrusion on the lower part of the front panel for fog lights.
(B.Ridgway)

August 1995 and one time GGPTE LA 1106 had become KCB 1910. Seen departing Buchanan Bus Station for Cumbernauld wearing KCB livery, the bus is covered in adverts, but where are the fleetnames? (B.Ridgway)

A heavily cannibalised LA 1442, above in SBL livery, sits inside the former Possilpark Garage in the summer of 2003, the First Greater Glasgow fleetnames having been applied over the Strathclyde Buses version. Also visible is LA 1285, the last panoramic Atlantean to see service in Glasgow. (Author)

Lying inside the former Bridgeton Bus Garage in the spring of 2003 is LA 1443. Still wearing First Glasgow red livery, restoration of this vehicle is finally underway after 5 years of lying around in a withdrawn condition. Also visible is LA 1448, the last new Atlantean for SPTE , and in the background one time Glasgow Titan L108. (Author)

Wan and two halves to the terminus drivar

The nineties were to prove a dramatic period for the Glasgow Atlantean. In the spring of 1992, after 2 years of negotiating, Strathclyde Regional Council accepted a bid of £ 28.1 million from a management employee buy-out team for the bus fleet. Had the sale been put on the open market it would no doubt have raised more money, and their bid was increased to £ 30.6 million before the Secretary of State for Scotland accepted it in November 1992. Despite hopes of an early conclusion to the deal, it was the 19th February 1993 before the sale was finalized. Besides the four garages at Knightswood, Larkfield, Parkhead and Posssilpark, the new owners also purchased 779 buses comprising 6 Ailsa B55, 111 Volvo B55, 100 Volvo Citybus, 6 Volvo B10M, 1 MCW Metroliner, 70 MCW Metrorider, 2 Optare Metrorider, 70 MCW Metrobus, 2 Leyland Leopard, 1 Leyland Tiger, 39 Leyland Olympian and the small matter of 371 Atlanteans. The Atlanteans comprising:-

LA 664/757/60/65/75/77/81/87/91/951/2/1030/34/43/49/52/97/99

1101/04/06/08-10/12/13/18/20-27/29-44/47/48/50-64/66-70/72-86/89-92/94-97/99

1200-12/14-19/21-37/39-1307/09-26/28-1400/02-06/08-20/23-29/32-83

The purchase of Kelvin Central Buses in 1994 and the proposed competitive services in Glasgow by Stagecoach in the same year, had a noticeable effect on both the size and deployment of SBL`s Atlantean fleet. The sale of Strathclyde Bus Holdings to First Group was to have the biggest impact on the remaining Atlanteans. SBL had already started to renew its fleet prior to selling to First, but the Atlantean appeared to still have a use in the foreseeable future. The approach by First was to be different and large numbers of new buses were soon ordered and operating in Glasgow. By the middle of 1997 the Glasgow Atlantean was in terminal decline, all three of the former SBH subsidiaries had diminishing numbers of Atlanteans in their fleets. Indeed the arrival of those new buses for First Glasgow was leading to the transfer of Atlanteans to other First Group companies throughout the UK for further service. It appeared, correctly as it turned out, that the Atlantean would be gone by the end of 1998. Rumours abounded that First Group was sending ten Glasgow Atlanteans, LA 1237/57/63/1304/34/42/49/1434/ 1441/1447, to Cuba for humanitarian work. In the end the closest that the Atlanteans got to Cuba was the Barnsley scrapyards, former Central Scottish Leyland Leopards, SL 247/48/55/57/64/66/69 /70/71 being sent from Glasgow in their place. What no one foresaw was the refusal of the Atlantean to go quietly, with First introducing a new livery in Glasgow that delayed the withdrawal of the type as the Atlanteans were needed to replace buses in for repaint. At the third attempt the Atlantean got its last running day in

June 1998, but even so Atlanteans were left to prowl the streets for another five months until time was called on LA 1408.

They may have been no more in Glasgow, but LA 12 34/54/60/72/1300/53/57/74 were sold by a dealer to the Chicago Coach Company of Illinois, USA during 1999. After three years in the windy city, the buses were sold for further use with operators in Florida, New Jersey, San Diego and Springfield Massachusetts. But for most folks, the Atlantean experience was now confined to bumping into one of the trainers as they toured the city on driver training or route familiarization duties.

All Atlantean buffs have their own memories of them but for the author, the Clyde Tunnel encapsulates the whole Atlantean experience, whether on the bus or following behind in a car. On entering the tunnel, the driver would lift off the power and down the slope the bus would run; just as the tunnel bottomed out the Leyland 680 engine, that beast under the bonnet, would explode into life as the task of powering the bus back to the surface began, raising a cacophony of thundering sound until the exit was reached! In Glasgow terms, magic, pure magic!

Lets not forget about the flute band Atlanteans. Externally they appeared just like the rest of the fleet, yet these AN68s had the uncanny knack to whistle just like the bands that every summer participate in orange walks around the West of Scotland! No one appears to be able to pin down the exact cause of this defect, although squealing gearboxes have been suggested, but it was peculiar to the orange, sorry red, Atlanteans that really were `orange` buses after all. Such was the notoriety of the `flute bands` that at least one reader was moved to write to the Glasgow Herald about the strange whistling buses that were roaming the city.

One of the strangest and certainly stupidest bus related things I have seen involved an Atlantean heading up Queen Margaret Drive in the West End. As the bus stopped at Hotspur Street two wee boys, aged nine or ten, jumped on the rear of the bus and grabbed hold of the handles on the insides of both engine pods. As the bus headed up the hill these two kids, one on each side of the bus, held on for dear life with their feet just reaching the bumper for extra support. When the bus stopped at the traffic lights at Maryhill Road a very irate driver suddenly appeared at the rear of the bus and in finest Glaswegian vernacular told the now rapidly disappearing, and lucky, waifs to relocate themselves to anywhere but the back of his bus!

Ultimately, two people are responsible for these memories of the Glasgow Atlantean, E.R.L. Fitzpayne and Alan Westwell. When Mr. Fitzpayne decided that Glasgow should purchase LA 1 back in 1958, no one could have foreseen the impact that the Atlantean was to have on the Glasgow fleet, let alone its impact on the British bus industry. That a troublesome PDR Atlantean fleet was built up towards the end of Mr Fitzpayne's stewardship of the Corporation bus fleet is without doubt. But it must be remembered that the Atlantean was the first rear engined chassis, so Leyland was going to make design mistakes with the Atlantean that other chassis makers would learn to avoid. Those early Atlanteans caused no end of problems and compared with the half cabs, were more time consuming to repair. It is easy with hindsight to question the wisdom in buying them, but technology is constantly evolving and the man who doesn't keep track of new developments is going to get left behind. Just as Concorde wouldn't have existed without the Wright brothers, today's rear engined buses with all their fancy gimmicks owe their existence, directly or not, to those early Atlanteans. If it hadn't been the Atlantean, it was only a matter of time before someone else produced a similar product. That Daimler brought out the Fleetline in the early sixties and Bristol the VR in the mid sixties, suggests that other chassis suppliers were aware of the threat the Atlantean posed to their traditional half cab markets. Whilst the Fleetline and VR were built in healthy numbers, neither came close to challenging the Atlantean as the leading seller amongst the first generation of rear engined buses. It is interesting to hear from operators who operated both Daimler Fleetlines and ex-Glasgow PDRs. Despite the problems associated with the Glasgow buses, they all preferred the Atlantean with the exception of one component, the Gardner engine that was supplied with the Fleetline. It is interesting to hear this, as the reason that the Scottish Bus Group bought Seddon Pennine saloons in the mid-seventies was because of Leyland's reluctance to put Gardner engines in the Leopard chassis. Whilst Glasgow did operate a Fleetline, they would also have operated VRs had Ronald Cox had his way. A cancelled order by the National Bus Company for 90 VRs led to them being offered to the PTE., Ronald Cox was happy to take the buses

but his Chief Engineer, Alan Westwell, wanted nothing to do with them. He felt that the operating environment in Glasgow was not suited to the VR and the fact that to take out the gearbox required the engine to be removed was labour and money intensive. With his Chief Engineer failing to endorse the VR, Mr Cox had little choice but to decline Leyland's offer. With Mr Cox's love of the panoramic body, would it have gone on the VRs?

There is no doubt those early Atlanteans were a challenge to keep on the road, but little could anyone have realised in 1972 that the incoming 32 year old Chief Engineer was to have a major impact on the bus fleet. Alan Westwell is rightly credited with sorting out the problems in the PDR Atlantean fleet that he inherited. What makes his approach so absorbing is that he didn't do things because he thought they should be done, he did things because he KNEW from getting his hands dirty they had to be done. That he believed that the Atlantean contained fundamental weaknesses within its design makes the amount of effort he put into these buses all the more remarkable. His return as Director General of the PTE in 1979 brought yet more tinkering with those troublesome Atlanteans. By now the panoramic bodies were starting to deteriorate and once again he set about ways to life extend buses that were

To commemorate the Glasgow Atlantean, First Glasgow produced this timetable in conjunction with the Atlantean running day in June 1998.

prematurely decaying. He not only changed the body style on those last 99 Atlanteans, but the plushest interiors seen on a Glasgow Atlantean replaced the dull green interiors of their predecessors. He didn't just confine his ideas to the Atlanteans however, little could the man in the street have realised just how deep his influence over the way the PTE operated its buses and services was. Just like those Metropolitans a decade earlier, Alan Westwell was trying things that wouldn't become mainstream in the bus industry for many years to come.

In all its guises from Glasgow Corporation to Strathclyde Buses, the company bought 1501 Atlanteans, 1449 of them new. Yet the feeling remains that the Atlantean was lucky to reach this total. If a single sourcing policy had been conducted between 1962 and 1984, when Merseyside PTE bought its last Atlantean, and adding in the second-hand buses then, 1827 Atlanteans would have been owned. However, let`s be realistic about this. What if the Scottish Bus Group had taken over the Corporation's bus fleet in the sixties? SBG settled on the lowheight Daimler Fleetline in the sixties when it bought rear engined buses. In the seventies, if Leyland had been able to get the Titan concept running earlier, the Atlantean would probably have ceased production sooner than it did. The Metropolitans were, sadly, just too advanced for their own good to be a long term threat and at a local level, Alan Westwell left for Tayside before the Ailsas got a chance to establish an influence on fleet purchases.

By 2005 there are very few former Glasgow Atlanteans surviving and those that remain will rely on the dedication and commitment of preservationists who are committed to the cause of commemorating Glasgow's omnibus heritage. It is sad that so few remain, but this indifference is not confined to just the Atlanteans, all the post 1960 chassis used by Glasgow are under represented in preservation. Is it indifference within the preservation movement, ignorance of the facts, or are Glasgow bus enthusiasts embarrassed by the fantastic bus heritage that Glasgow's bus operators have built up? It is hard to define the exact cause, but when one sees the pride that other UK cities, especially Manchester, have taken in their bus fleet, it is something that has to be rectified, and quickly.

The Glasgow Atlantean could best be described as a swan. The public image was graceful lines and fine liveries, but out of sight there was frantic activity just to keep them roadworthy. Whilst the evidence implies that the Glasgow Atlantean will not be remembered as the best bus ever, it had its fans and already it is missed by enthusiasts. Indeed had the Atlantean been perfect and super reliable, it probably would not have been half as interesting. The fact that so many buses underwent alterations and modifications gave the fleet character and added enormous interest for enthusiasts. It is interesting to note just how many Glaswegians, although not knowing an Atlantean from a Metrobus, will see an image of an Alexander `AL` Atlantean and associate it with a Glasgow bus. One wonders if in 25 years, will any of the current chassis available to operators evoke such emotion amongst future generations of bus enthusiasts and the Glasgow public? I know my answer, what is yours?

In the autumn of 2005, Lothian's last Atlantean in service (659) was in temporary storage at the Bus World museum in Hillington. In the above image Glasgow's last Atlantean in service (LA 1408) and 659 provide an interesting comparison between two buses that share a common body style. (Author)